"I pray almost every day that the Lord would create in me a greater hunger for his word and his ways. But for that to happen my appetites must be reoriented. In *Help for the Hungry Soul*, Kristen Wetherell reveals our deepest hunger pains as she points us to the only source of true satisfaction. So pick up this book, and you will taste and see that the Lord is good."

Courtney Doctor, Director of Women's Initiatives, The Gospel Coalition; Bible teacher; author, *From Garden to Glory* and *In View of God's Mercies*

"*Help for the Hungry Soul* serves as an encouragement to all of us, regardless of the season we are in, that God himself delights in arousing, sustaining, and satisfying our spiritual hungers by giving us the gift of his word and his presence. These short, content-rich chapters will encourage you afresh that God delights in filling the hungry with good things (Ps. 107)."

Amy Gannett, Founder and Creator, Tiny Theologians; Writer and Bible Teacher, The Bible Study Schoolhouse; author, *Fix Your Eyes*

"In *Help for the Hungry Soul*, Kristen Wetherell has found a way to champion the habit of Bible reading without the frequent side effects of guilt or legalism. She invites us to dig deeper into God's precious word while also freeing us from the obligatory 'quiet time.' This book is a hope-filled encouragement to those who long for more of God and yet constantly feel unable to find the time or energy to follow through."

Kelly Needham, wife; mom of five; author, *Friendish* and *Purposefooled*

"This book is more than a good read. It's a life-changer that will increase your hunger for God's word. Honest, personal stories from real people will enable you to identify with their struggles to grow in his word. Kristen Wetherell's insights increase my commitment to pray for each of my twenty-one grandchildren to fall in love with the word of God (Ps. 119:105)."

Susan Alexander Yates, speaker; blogger, SusanAlexanderYates. com; author, *Risky Faith* and *One Devotional*

"'Gather a day's portion.' That's a truth I love to rehearse in the morning as I open up the Bible and ask for God's help. It's a reminder I don't need to do too much in morning devotions—and I need to make sure to do the main thing. And it's a feeding image—a picture of hunger and eating and satisfaction. Of the many good ways we can approach reading, studying, and meditating on God's word, the feeding image is as important—and practically helpful—as any. That's why I love the vision of this book: to grow your soul's appetite for God through his word. Kristen Wetherell is both a skilled and reliable guide. So take up and read yourself into greater hunger and feed afresh on the only one who truly satisfies."

David Mathis, Senior Teacher and Executive Editor, desiringGod. org; Pastor, Cities Church, Saint Paul, Minnesota; author, *Habits of Grace*

"Reading *Help for the Hungry Soul* will be a ministry of grace to you. Not only will this book stir your appetite for the deep things of God, but it will also give you a satisfying and nourishing meal along the way."

Jared C. Wilson, Assistant Professor of Pastoral Ministry and Author in Residence, Midwestern Baptist Theological Seminary; author, *The Imperfect Disciple* and *Love Me Anyway*

"At last! A book that is full of encouragement in an area where many Christians feel only defeat. *Help for the Hungry Soul* will stir your heart to feed on God's word. It will entice you with the *why* and equip you with the *how*."

Colin Smith, Senior Pastor, The Orchard, Arlington Heights, Illinois; Founder and Bible Teacher, Open the Bible

Help for the Hungry Soul

Help for the Hungry Soul

*Eight Encouragements to Grow Your
Appetite for God's Word*

Kristen Wetherell

Foreword by Jani Ortlund

CROSSWAY®

WHEATON, ILLINOIS

Help for the Hungry Soul: Eight Encouragements to Grow Your Appetite for God's Word

Copyright © 2023 by Kristen Wetherell

Published by Crossway
        1300 Crescent Street
        Wheaton, Illinois 60187

Cover and illustration design: Crystal Courtney

First printing 2023

Printed in the United States of America

Hardcover ISBN: 978-1-4335-8861-7
ePub ISBN: 978-1-4335-8864-8
PDF ISBN: 978-1-4335-8862-4

Library of Congress Cataloging-in-Publication Data

Names: Wetherell, Kristen, author.
Title: Help for the hungry soul : eight encouragements to grow your appetite for God's word / Kristen Wetherell.
Description: Wheaton, Illinois : Crossway, 2023. | Includes bibliographical references and index.
Identifiers: LCCN 2022047904 (print) | LCCN 2022047905 (ebook) | ISBN 9781433588617 (hardcover) | ISBN 9781433588624 (pdf) | ISBN 9781433588648 (epub)
Subjects: LCSH: Bible—Study and Teaching. | Christian life.
Classification: LCC BS600.3 .W48 2023 (print) | LCC BS600.3 (ebook) | DDC 220.07—dc23/eng/20230320
LC record available at https://lccn.loc.gov/2022047904
LC ebook record available at https://lccn.loc.gov/2022047905

Crossway is a publishing ministry of Good News Publishers.

To all the saints in Jesus Christ who are at The Orchard,
who trust, proclaim, preach, teach, study, read,
love, and hunger for God's word:
may you grow deeper roots, richer life, and more fruit.
I thank my God in all my remembrance of you (Phil. 1:3).

Contents

Open your mouth wide, and I will fill it.

PSALM 81:10

Foreword

APPARENTLY, I WAS A VERY FUSSY EATER as a baby. My pediatrician insinuated that my mother was not trying hard enough to get her eighteen-month-old daughter to eat, and Mom was distressed. She determined to get me to eat more. "Come on, darling. Open up! This tastes yummy. Try it—you'll like it!" But have you ever tried to get a fussy toddler to open her mouth and take in what you know she needs? It is pretty much impossible to pry open little jaws that are firmly clenched shut in a picky protest. And even if you could force in a little bite of nourishment, how would you get her to swallow it?

Fortunately, I'm not such a fussy eater these days. I love all kinds of foods and, surprisingly enough, find myself willing to try new ones. In fact, I've even come to enjoy the venison and elk my dear Ray fills our freezer with each fall. It's a good thing I have a healthy appetite!

In *Help for the Hungry Soul*, Kristen Wetherell shows us how God uses our natural physical hunger to teach us about our supernatural spiritual hunger for him. Just as we can starve our bodies, we can also starve our souls. And if we refuse his soul food, he won't force-feed us. That's really scary. After all, whose spiritual appetite stays consistently strong week after week, month after month? We need help.

Kristen helps us see that God himself arouses, sustains, and satisfies our deepest hunger. I love her short, clear chapters with engaging stories of hungry souls feasting at the table of the King. She shows us how eager our heavenly Father is to satisfy our soul hunger. "The hungry soul he fills with good things" (Ps. 107:9). My affection for God's word has been renewed as Kristen helped me fall more deeply in love with Christ himself, the living Word.

That's why I'm grateful for this book. Kristen understands the wonder it is to go from hindered to hopeful, from dulled to delighted, from picky to passionate. She calls this wonder the *miracle* of loving God's word. And she guides us in *how* to bring our fussy hearts to our kind King for him to work that miracle in us.

Help for the Hungry Soul is an enticing invitation to every one of us to slow down and feast on the bread of life (John 6:48). I hope you'll accept this invitation to "open your mouth wide" and let him fill it. You'll be glad you did. Now—let the feasting begin!

Jani Ortlund

RENEWAL MINISTRIES

Why do you spend your money for that which is not bread,
and your labor for that which does not satisfy?
Listen diligently to me, and eat what is good,
and delight yourselves in rich food.

Jesus said to them, "I am the bread of life;
whoever comes to me shall not hunger, and
whoever believes in me shall never thirst."

JOHN 6:35

Nothing can make us hungry for Scripture
more than Scripture itself.

DONALD S. WHITNEY
Ten Questions to Diagnose Your Spiritual Health

Introduction

A Hunger to Hear from God

I WROTE THIS BOOK because I am hungry, and I know I'm not alone.

Look around you. Beneath the digital cries for attention is hunger. Lurking under the nagging sense of not-enoughness is hunger. Lingering beside the longing for more is hunger.

Hunger is everywhere. It is within you and within me.

You know it. It's that insatiable craving for more that not even the biggest promotion or highest honor can curb. It's that unsettled feeling that all is not right with the world, even after the best and brightest day, and that there is more to be enjoyed and more rest to be found. It's the grumble of discontentment that keeps us hopping from one thing to the next as we think, *There must be more to life than this.*

And yet, we settle for less.

I wonder how many of us know what it is to feed these hunger pangs, the crying-out of our souls, with food that doesn't ultimately satisfy or nourish us. That's why I wrote this book—a book about food.

Well, sort of.

Help for the Hungry Soul is ultimately a book about your soul, and the food your soul needs to live.

Born to Hunger

I was born hungry. So were you.

Think about it: What is the purpose of an appetite? If we had no appetite, we wouldn't know the loveliness of eating food. Appetite is beneficial; it leads us to seek what we need to survive and thrive. It is our body's cry for help, a God-given alarm system for our flourishing.

A person with a skewed appetite (or no appetite) is a person whose body is unwell.

The same goes for your soul. Have you considered that it was also created with an appetite? You were made to desire and hunger for your eternal Creator (Gen. 1:26–27; Eccles. 3:11; Isa. 55:6–7; Mic. 6:8; John 15:5). Man and woman (you and I) were fashioned to reflect the God whose existence never ends, as our Creator breathed the breath of life—*God's* very life—into Adam's nostrils and planted the tree of life beside him in the garden (Gen. 2:7–9). It has always been God's delight to share his life with us.

Our souls were made to live forever, feasting always on his goodness.

And so, in a moment of great opportunity, what did the serpent use to tempt Eve to disobedience? He used appetite, *hunger*.

God had given Adam and Eve the freedom to eat from every tree in the garden except one (Gen. 2:9, 16–17). *Just one*. Every other tree would sustain them, but the evil tree would destroy them, body and soul. The enemy used a familiar instinct—a good, God-given instinct—to deceive and kill. Our first parents ate, and they would never be the same. Neither would we.

The Word at the beginning who made them hungry for him, who made them to live with him forever, had spoken clear words for Adam and Eve to live by. But they chose different words and listened to a different voice (Gen. 3:11, 17). They fed themselves with lies, and they died.

Body and soul, they perished in their sin.

Now, thanks to Adam and Eve, our appetites have gone terribly wrong. We are still as hungry as ever—but for the wrong things. And so, from the garden throughout the generations we have dealt with our soul-hunger in manifold, creative, yet unsuccessful ways. How God has dealt with it, however, has been quite simple and straightforward.

He has spoken. "Man shall not live by bread alone, / but by every word that comes from the mouth of God" (Matt. 4:4; see Deut. 8:3).

Many People Are "Hungry"

This is a book about God's word, but it's not a *how-to*—there are lots of excellent books about Bible reading and study methods. Here, I write about the *why*, the heart behind opening our Bibles. I want to help the person who feels stuck and defeated.

So, yes, this is a book about food, but of a different category. It is about the life-giving nourishment God has graciously provided for his hungry, starving people throughout the ages: his word. I am praying that *Help for the Hungry Soul* will freshly entice you to feast on true food, the living words of the living God who alone can sustain and satisfy your eternal hunger with himself.

Now, you may be thinking, *That's great, Kristen. Bible reading might come easily to you, but it's hard for me. I know I'm supposed to, but I have little desire for it. I'll never be where other Christians are, where I should be.*

In truth, my heart is in a similar position as yours. Just when I thought I would be writing this book from a place of relative strength, I was thrust into the reality of my weakness. I was reawakened to my need for grace. I was reminded that all of us are dependent on the Lord to make us more hungry for him.

If you think you're alone in not wanting to read your Bible, think differently. A recent article about American Bible reading habits says, "Relatively few Americans—including Christians—read the Bible often." Only one in six adults reads the Bible most days during the week.[1]

This finding confirms what I've heard from many people over the last year. Through surveying various groups and talking to friends, church leaders, and pastors, by far the most common word used to describe people's appetites for God's word is *hungry*, yet this takes on different tones in different contexts. Some have said their hunger is a deep and ever-increasing desire for Scripture (praise God for that), while many others have used *hunger* to describe a languishing or longing of the soul.

---

1   See Joe Carter, "When We Don't Delight in Reading Scripture," *The Gospel Coalition*, May 15, 2021, https://www.thegospelcoalition.org/.

People are hungry—but not hungry enough to engage.

People are hungry—but not sure what to do about it.

People are hungry—but for things other than God's word.

Revival and Reorientation

How would you describe your current appetite for God's word? Maybe it has been years since you've opened a Bible, or maybe you've never read it before. Perhaps you engage with Scripture consistently, but your heart feels flat to it, and you've grown discouraged. Maybe Bible reading has seemed like more of a "supposed to" than a "want to," and you're not convinced you could feel differently. Or maybe the desire is there, but you struggle to act on it.

It seems to me that the church needs a revival of hunger for the living words of the living God—a compelling answer to the question, *How can I love Scripture again?*—as well as a reorientation about what engaging with God's word actually looks like for hungry people with full lives.

We need a stirring up and a settling down.

As we'll see, the stirring up of the human heart isn't a formula but a supernatural gift.[2] In other words, the right spiritual food doesn't necessarily *equal* spiritual appetite. A person can engage with God's words by reading or hearing them and remain hardened, as Jesus talks about in his parable of the sower (Matt. 13:1–23).

But we also can't expect our appetites to grow if we aren't feeding on soul-food. There is a connection between consuming

2   More on this in chapter 2.

God's words and loving God's words. And yet, we also need his direct, divine intervention. *We need him.* As pastor and author John Piper says:

> The act of reading, in order to be done as God intended, must be done in dependence on God's supernatural help. . . . If more people approached the Bible with a deep sense of helplessness, and hope-filled reliance on God's merciful assistance, there would be far more seeing and savoring and transformation than there is.[3]

The stirring up of our souls is something only God can do—and is anything too hard for him (Jer. 32:27)? As you read this book, my hope is that God will use it to this end, that he will whet your appetite for his word as we explore the questions *Why should I love Scripture?* and *How is it possible for me to desire it again?* I pray that by the end you will be refreshed and compelled to feast on his living words in a new way. I pray that, right this moment, you will open yourself up to this supernatural possibility, however apathetic or discouraged you may feel.

But we not only need a stirring up; we also need a settling down.

I don't mean "we need to settle" (far from it!). I mean *we need to rest* in the many amazing opportunities and contexts we have to consume God's word, rather than constantly feeling guilty about not having perfect daily devotions—what we have come to know as "quiet time."

3   John Piper, *Reading the Bible Supernaturally* (Wheaton, IL: Crossway, 2017), 183–84.

Daily quiet time is not bad or wrong! It is, in fact, a very good habit. But we need a reorientation about what loving God's word actually looks like for hungry people with full lives; we need *biblical* reorientation, rather than trying to mimic historical or cultural ideals. Ultimately, we need to combat false guilt from narrow notions about what it means to feast on God's words and rest in God's kindness to give us ample opportunities to enjoy Scripture.

In other words, it's possible you're not failing in this area as much as you think you are. I believe we will be encouraged by what we discover.

A Hunger to Hear from God

The brief chapters that follow are eight encouragements for growing an appetite for God's word, the everlasting food your soul needs most. Some of these will take us back to the basics, reminding us of truths we may have forgotten or taken for granted. Others will give us a fresh perspective on what it looks like to engage practically with Scripture.

You can read the chapters in the order they are written, or jump around as you see fit (although they do build on one another). Each one ends with an application section with exercises and other prompts that I hope will be useful to you. Above all, I encourage you to have your Bible beside you as you read, to let this book drive you to *the* book.

Woven throughout, you'll also find short testimonies written by other believers, in various life stages and vocations, about how God has increased their appetite for his words. I hope these stories will encourage you to pursue a Bible-nourished life.

So, what do you say? Will you receive God's invitation to listen diligently to him, eat what is good, and delight yourselves in rich food (Isa. 55:2)? Might I be so bold as to whet your appetite for God's soul-nourishing words of life? My challenge to you is to read to the end and see if his Spirit hasn't stirred in your heart, even to a small degree, a longing for more— a hunger to hear from him.

O LORD, you have searched me and known me!

PSALM 139:1

*Let us search our ways and find out how
matters stand between ourselves and God.*

J. C. RYLE
Practical Religion

*For he satisfies the longing soul,
and the hungry soul he fills with good things.*

PSALM 107:9

1

Know Your Hungry Heart

I STOOD BEFORE a room full of women from a local church who had gathered for a weekend retreat. For the past three days, I had had the great joy of teaching them from God's word and connecting with them in conversation. These women loved the Lord and one another, and were clearly hungry to learn from Scripture together—so hungry that they had committed an entire weekend to this pursuit. I hadn't planned on surveying them for this book, but after the last session I asked them if they would be willing to answer a few questions for me.

Their insights have been invaluable (thank you, sisters!). One of the questions I asked—the one that seemed most important and revealing—was, *How would you describe your current appetite for God's word?*

By far, the most common answer was *hungry*.

Three Kinds of Biblical Hunger

My question for you right now is the same: How would you describe your current appetite for God's word?

My aim in this chapter is to help you know yourself better so you can discern how you might grow. I'm praying that God, by his Spirit, will help us understand our hungry hearts, what we are desiring most, and how those desires play out on a normal day as they relate to God's word. Think of this chapter as a kind of "heart check."

First, we will look at three kinds of biblical hunger and consider which one best applies to us. Then we will look at five common hindrances that can keep us from growing an appetite for Scripture. Ready? Let's begin.

Starving Hunger

First, there's the starving hunger of a heart that is always hungry but never satisfied. God says this is like trying to fill up a broken, holey jar with water:

> For my people have committed two evils:
>   they have forsaken me,
>   the fountain of living waters,
> and hewed out cisterns for themselves,
>   broken cisterns that can hold no water. (Jer. 2:13)

This is every human being's natural condition, as we seek to feed our hunger with what can never satisfy us (Isa. 55:2). It is a useless and exhausting way to live.

On its own efforts, the human heart remains empty and starving. It will always be searching for satisfaction in the wrong places—unless God himself rescues us.

Perhaps this description feels too close to home. Perhaps you have found yourself desperate to be satisfied in your deepest heart, but nothing in this world has been able to do this for you. There is good news: *You were made for more. You were made for God, for fullest satisfaction in him.*

Your Creator is also the Redeemer of the starving heart. In every way that the world has come up empty to you, you can count on him being the fullness your soul most hungers for. Why not ask him, even right now? He will delight to answer your hungry call, filling you with his Spirit and changing what you love (Pss. 14:2; 145:18).

Seeking Hunger

Have you gone through seasons when God seems far away and you have little desire for him? You know the Lord is the only true fulfillment for the longing of your soul, but reading your Bible feels dull and dry. My hand is raised. I've lost count of the times I've experienced this and have now come to expect these seasons. They are part of the normal Christian experience.

Are you there right now? Know you are not alone. In fact, your desire to keep seeking God proves the genuineness of your hunger for him (1 Pet. 1:6–7). Only those who love the Lord want more of him when he feels distant (Pss. 27; 63). Only those who have tasted and seen his goodness know when that taste wanes (Ps. 34:8).

Why do we experience these seasons? We will look more carefully at five specific reasons below, but certain factors leave us feeling far from God and hungering for more of him, such as physical and mental exhaustion, suffering, struggles with sin patterns, distraction, and God's purposeful withdrawing so our hunger for him will grow.[1]

Whatever your situation, hear God's promise to you as you seek him: "I love those who love me, / and those who seek me diligently find me" (Prov. 8:17).

Satisfied Hunger

Finally, there is the holy hunger of the satisfied heart. Over the past several months, I have grown to love Psalm 119, which might be the best example of this kind of hunger. The psalm is a complex and honest heart cry of hunger to know and rejoice in God and his words—the kind of hunger that every believer in Jesus has the privilege of knowing, in some form and degree, because of his intervening, transforming grace.

Notice the complexity and realism in the psalmist's words:

My soul clings to the dust;
　　give me life according to your word!
When I told of my ways, you answered me;
　　teach me your statutes!
Make me understand the way of your precepts,
　　and I will meditate on your wondrous works. . . .
I cling to your testimonies, O LORD;
　　let me not be put to shame!

1　The Puritans called these "God's desertions," times when God withholds from us a perceived sense of his presence (although he never actually leaves us). See Donald S. Whitney, *Ten Questions to Diagnose Your Spiritual Health* (Colorado Springs: NavPress, 2021), 10.

I will run in the way of your commandments
  when you enlarge my heart! (Ps. 119:25–27, 31–32)

The psalmist plays his song from heartstrings deeply rehearsed in God's character, ways, and words, for he knows the Lord and wants more of him; and yet, at the same time, he plays a *realistic* song. He has learned to hunger for God all the more because life is hard and his heart is wayward—but God is entirely trustworthy.

Right there is the blessing of true Godward hunger: *the more of God we come to know, the more of God we want to know.* This doesn't mean perfection, for all our yearnings in this life will be incomplete until we see Jesus; but it does mean we have endless potential to grow, as we seek more of God and receive the fullness of joy that only he can give (Ps. 16:11).

We long to be satisfied in him and in his precious words.

Five Common Hindrances to Bible Reading

At this point, you may want to turn to the final section of this chapter ("Knowing Your Hungry Heart"), where you'll see a couple of exercises to help you process what kind of hunger you are currently experiencing. Feel free to fill out your responses now. When you're ready, continue reading here.

What often keeps us from engaging with Scripture? See how many of these five hindrances apply to you.

1. Distraction

We are living in an age of unparalleled opportunities and unrelenting stimulation, when the influence of technology has greatly affected our desire and ability to receive God's word. The digital hubbub has rewired our brains, making us obsessed with noise and newness, addicted to instant gratification, and unable to focus, all of which can make hearing and reading God's word—a practice that is helped by concentration, commitment, and quiet—difficult.

You know the scenario. You're thinking about a Bible passage or a recent sermon, only to find your thoughts wandering about that work project you have to finish or that recent debate you heard online (which causes you to check your phone again). Hello, distraction.

How have you seen technology's influence become dangerous to your walk with God? How have you seen the enemy use it to keep you from God and his life-giving word (Mark 4:15)? Distraction is one pervasive hindrance we'll want to be aware of as we seek to grow.

2. Dullness

Technological and cultural advances have lavished us with an abundance of Bible resources. These are gifts from God that can stir our hunger for him. But sometimes they have the opposite effect: we take them for granted and become bored with what feels overfamiliar.[2] As pastor and author J. C. Ryle says, "We hardly know the value of the air we breathe, and the sun which shines on us, because we have never known what it is to be without them."[3] Dullness of heart can especially affect those who have become well-acquainted with the Bible, like

2   More on this in chapter 4.
3   J. C. Ryle, *Practical Religion* (Edinburgh: Banner of Truth, 2013), 98.

pastors, seminary students, and Bible teachers. I'm talking about myself here.

What might this look like? Perhaps it becomes easy for us to approach our Bibles as a mere duty rather than as communion with the living God (John 5:39–40). Dullness may cause us to forget that we don't actually deserve to hear from God at all, and it might tempt us to look for extrabiblical revelation, as if hearing from God directly through Scripture isn't enough for us. We need to be on guard for hearts that have become dull to the word of life.

3. Deceit

Our hearts can also be deceived into believing lies about God and his word. This is one of Satan's greatest tactics as the father of lies (John 8:44). Even for believers in Jesus whose hearts have been set free by his truth (John 8:32), the temptation toward deceit is real.

That said, we can ask God to make us aware of untrue thoughts that distract us from God's word and dull our hearts to his beauty, authority, and power. What might these lies sound like? Rather than believe that God is loving us well through his words, we suspect the Bible contains only *rules and restraints that limit and condemn us*. Rather than trust what God says, distrusting our own fallen wisdom in favor of his perfection, *we question and doubt him*. Rather than hunger for eternal realities and love what God loves, we are deceived into *settling for worldly values and ideals*, thinking they will make us happy.

We are at war. The Christian life is a great battle for the heart as we put off deceit and let the truth set us free from it—which is why we need the word.

4. Discouragement

What has made it hard for you to endure, or what has sent you into seasons of spiritual dryness? Maybe you haven't opened your Bible for months because your newborn has kept you up all night for equally as long. Maybe your aging parents need you constantly, draining your tank of whatever might have been left for the Lord. Or maybe Bible reading feels more like a chore to complete than a blessing to enjoy.

Perhaps you're in the midst of a kind of suffering you never saw coming: illness, chronic pain, depression, grief, and other trials that make it hard to get out of bed in the morning, let alone invest energy in God's word. Our pain fills our heads, weighs on our hearts, and tempts us toward discouragement and apathy.

Jesus also notes persecution "on account of the word" (Mark 4:17). When we choose to follow him, there are uncomfortable costs (Mark 8:38), whether we are sacrificing our reputations or finding our very lives in danger. People of the world will think we are crazy for being people of the book.

We *will* be discouraged from walking with God in this fallen world. The question is, Will we allow these discouragements to drive us to his word or away from it?

5. Desires

We don't always want what's good for us (vegetables and exercise, anyone?). Wrong desires can also hinder us from hungering for God's word—and not only that, they can kill us slowly as our hearts shrivel under their influence. If we are outrightly living in sinful practices (1 John 2:16), there will be no room in our hearts for God and his word (James 4:4).

But what about those of us who desire to love and please God, but don't always want what's good for our souls? We no longer live in sinful practices, but we still war against sin's presence and wrong desires (Rom. 7:21–25). This fight can affect our hunger for the word.

Sometimes good things can replace God, as they take priority over him and become the pattern for our days. What "good-desires-turned-idols" have hindered you from enjoying God in his word? That extra hour of sleep that becomes a habit, leaving no time to read the Bible? The desire to make more money, which leads to working more hours, which leaves you too exhausted for anything else? The ease of regularly opening Netflix or social media, rather than seeking a better rest in the words of life?

This isn't to say that extra sleep, working hard, and entertainment are necessarily wrong (although they could be). But we want closeness with God to be the priority and pattern of our days, rather than the cares of the world and the desires of our flesh.

Pursuing Hungry Hearts

With these five hindrances in mind, at this point you may be feeling disheartened. If you're like me, you're thinking, *I struggle with most of these often, if not all the time.*

But remember our goal. We want our appetites for God's word to grow so our hearts are increasingly satisfied in him.

We need to acknowledge these hindrances—distraction, dullness, deceit, discouragement, and desires—so that, with God's help, we can begin to throw off anything that would keep us from loving his words. We long to look instead to Jesus, receiving his words with faith (Heb. 12:1–2) and growing in deeper hunger for him (John 6:35).

This is the goal, friends, and it's where we are headed in the rest of this book.

But how do we get there?

The reality is, none of us can attain this on our own. But Jesus is the Creator and Redeemer of our hearts, and therefore we are never without hope for change. The only way our affections for him will grow is if he gives growth (1 Cor. 3:6). The only way we will ever learn to love his words above all else is if he places such a love within us (Jer. 31:33). And the only way we will find our hunger for him changed—*and our hearts increasingly satisfied*—is if we plead with him to do what only he can do (Ps. 107:9): a miracle.

Knowing Your Hungry Heart

1. How would you describe your current appetite for God's word? Circle the words that resonate most with you right now. There are no right answers, just honest ones.

Indifferent	Anxious
Eager	Distracted
Overwhelmed	Bored
Desirous	Consistent
Sporadic	Craving

Longing	Strong
Disappointed	Nervous
Guilty	Hopeful
Desperate	Curious
Parched	Lazy
Thankful	Struggling
Lacking	Skeptical

2. On a scale of 0–10, how hungry are you to hear from the Lord?

3. Which of the three types of hunger best describes you right now? Why do you think this is?

4. Use the table below to determine which hindrances are currently keeping you from engaging with God. Start by reflecting on your habits associated with each hindrance. Don't hold back; get them all down on paper. Then in the third column, write down what you would like to see change so that God's word becomes more central in your days and heart.

Hindrances to Bible Reading

Hindrances	Current Habits	Potential Changes
Distraction		
Dullness		
Deceit		
Discouragement		
Desires		

A Growing Affection for God's Word

Lydia (forties, wife, mother, and women's discipleship codirector)

I grew up in the church. I was a pastor's kid, both of my grandfathers were pastors, and I attended a Christian grade school, a Christian high school, and a Christian college. I participated in AWANA, Sunday school, and youth group. I often won sword drill games or Bible trivia. I knew a lot about the Bible, and I knew a lot of theology and doctrine. But I don't think I could say with the psalmist, "Your law is my delight" (Ps. 119:174), or with Jesus, "Man shall not live by bread alone, / but by every word that comes from the mouth of God" (Matt. 4:4).

In truth, I did not love God's word. It was not what fed my soul. It was part of my life, but I held no affection for it. Until recently.

My affections for God's word shifted as I began to regularly participate in the women's Bible study at my church, then even more so when I was asked to help lead one of the Bible study small groups. In addition to my knowledge of the word increasing and my understanding being sharpened, my affection for the word of God deepened significantly. My affection for Christ is now richer. By God's grace, the help of the Holy Spirit, and the day-to-day transformative power of the gospel, I am different, and I attribute studying his word to playing a major role in that.

Another influence on my affection for the Bible happened in the spring and summer of 2020, during the COVID-19 pandemic. Author and podcaster Abbey Wedgeworth curated an Instagram series called "Significant Psalms," where she invited other women to share how a specific psalm had formed and impacted them. As I listened to each woman speak the truth about God, his character, his love, and his care for his people, my heart was drawn to the Psalms so deeply that I started reading one psalm a day. I quickly included my young children, and every morning at breakfast we read through a psalm together. Then after finishing the Psalms, we moved on to Proverbs, Luke, and Acts, and we have continued to read through other parts of the Bible together.

Incline my heart to your testimonies . . . !

PSALM 119:36

God never sets a man longing for mercy
without intending to give it.

CHARLES SPURGEON
"The Parable of the Sower"

But he would feed you with the finest of the wheat,
and with honey from the rock I would satisfy you.

PSALM 81:16

2

Plead for a Holy Hunger

WE LOVE MIRACLES. They surprise and excite us. Temporarily distracting us from our so-called uneventful existence, they make us feel connected, however ambiguously, to the divine. When a baby is born healthy and strong? "It's a miracle," we say. The rescue of an entire Thai soccer team from entrapment in a flooded cave? Miraculous.

Miracles, miracles everywhere—or so we think. We love remarkable events, even if they're not really miracles.

What if I told you that you could experience an actual miracle—a supernatural act of God—today? And what if I told you that this involves opening your Bible?

When I first encountered this argument, I had to pick my jaw up from the floor. After decades of studying my Bible, I read John Piper's wonderful book *Reading the Bible Supernaturally*, and my whole outlook on Scripture changed.[1]

---

1   I am deeply grateful to God for John Piper's excellent writing and faithful ministry, which God has used to deepen my hunger for him and his word.

Pastor John amazed me by this perspective-shifting reality: *to love God's word is a miracle.*

Our Hope for Hunger

In the last chapter, our aim was to do a heart check and examine our current appetite for God's word. We looked at several hindrances that can keep us from loving and hungering for it: distraction, dullness, deceit, discouragement, and desires. If you're like me, identifying these hindrances might have left you with some pressing questions.

If these can keep us from a greater, deeper hunger for God and his nourishing words, then what is our hope for growth?

Is satisfied hunger even possible for believers living in this fallen world?

And if it is possible, then how?

We will draw out the answers to these questions throughout the rest of this book. But the simple answer is that *our God is the initiator of the impossible* (Luke 1:37). Nothing is too hard for him (Gen. 18:14; Jer. 32:27)—even working on the complex and lukewarm hearts of wayward, skeptical, too-easily-satisfied people like you and me.

Our God is not dangling the proverbial carrot here, friends. If he invites us to find satisfaction in him, then he will make good on his invitation (Ps. 81:16; Isa. 55:1). He intends to fulfill his word as we earnestly seek him through his word. Our hope for hunger, then, is found in the one who beckons us to himself—particularly in *the miracle of spiritual hunger* that God alone can create within us, through his Spirit, as he awakens us to our helplessness and humbles us to our need.

Ready to Receive

"I *need* milk, Mommy!"

Thus goes the daily refrain of our two-year-old son as he pleads for milk before bed. Sometimes I remind him that he doesn't need milk—he *wants* it—but generally, I am touched by his childlike dependence on me, his momma, for something as simple as a cup of milk.

We too are needy, friends. Especially when it comes to our Bibles.

I want us, right now, to feel the wonderful freedom of this reality in our bones: only God can produce hunger within us for his words. This means that all our attempts to "read the Bible well enough" or "do what we're supposed to" or "feel all the right things" cannot *on their own* stir up within our hearts the hunger we so desire.

Here's what I mean. God often accomplishes his miraculous works through *means*, and we know his Spirit works through his words.[2] But in order for his Spirit to work through his words, we need to actually engage with those words. We need to *hear* God's word and *read* God's word.

We need to put ourselves in the blessed position to receive from God. *We need to be needy.*

In future chapters, we will talk more about the many practical and creative ways we might do this; but for now, settle it in your mind and heart that God does the impossible through very normal, everyday encounters with a book—his word.

---

2   This is why spiritual disciplines, like Bible reading and prayer, are often called "means of grace."

Only God can produce hunger within us for his words, but we can put ourselves in the blessed position to receive from him.

Speaking of little ones, Peter tells us to think and act like babies: "Like newborn infants, long for the pure spiritual milk, that by it you may grow up into salvation—if indeed you have tasted that the Lord is good" (1 Pet. 2:2–3). Newborns don't produce the milk their bodies need to grow and thrive; their moms do. But in order to benefit from their mothers' milk, those babies must be in a ready position to receive it. Like "newborn infants," then, we see our ongoing need for God to sustain us, and so we put ourselves in the way of *being sustained* by him (Phil. 2:12–13).

We open our Bible, and we plead with God to do what only he can do through it.

Why We Plead: We Are Helpless

Many of us know what it's like to feel defeated in our Bible reading before we even start. The desire just isn't there (or it isn't very strong). So we trudge down the stairs in the morning, grab a cup of coffee, and intend to sit down and read . . . only to find the vibration on our phones too intriguing, or the quickly accumulating mental list too pressing, or the needs and noise of our little kids too distracting.

We know what it's like to prefer other things, and then to *choose* those things. And most days, it's not a fight. It's an easy choice.

These common scenarios expose the deeper problem within our hearts: without the Spirit, we are helpless to want what we ought to want and to love what we ought to love. By nature, our hearts are twisted by sin, deceived into thinking that other things are more satisfying than God (Rom. 1:21–22). We do not want what is naturally best for us.

My husband and I enjoy watching the show *Alone*, where skilled survivalists are dropped in remote parts of the world and attempt to outlast the others. Those who trap, hunt, and catch the most food tend to survive the longest, but they all reach the point of starvation. And starvation changes the appetite. Interestingly enough, rather than wanting normal food and eating patterns, their intense hunger ends up completely changing what their bodies want.

What they need most, they don't desire.

Similarly, we are dependent on the Redeemer of our hearts to change our very desires, to give us the ability to want what we ought to want and to love what he loves. We are helpless to produce this change on our own. Day by day, we need him to alter our appetite.

But please don't hear me say that our helplessness excuses us from holiness. Far from it.

Remember that only God can produce hunger within us for his words, but we *can* put ourselves in the blessed position to receive from him. We can let our helplessness propel us into a posture of desperate need before the Holy Spirit, as we choose to open our Bibles and proceed in total and complete reliance on him.

Our helplessness humbles us.

How We Plead: We Are Humbled

Let's keep going with the illustration of children. Peter tells us to be like newborn infants, putting ourselves in a position to receive, and Jesus says something similar by telling us to become like little kids: "Truly, I say to you, unless you turn and become like children, you will never enter the kingdom of heaven" (Matt. 18:3). What are children like?

They can do very little for themselves. Most of the time, they know their limits and call upon those more capable for help. They make no pretenses, wearing their emotions on their sleeves. And they return to their parents again and again (and again), asking for what they want and need.

"I *need* milk, Mommy!"

In Jeremy Pierre's lovely words,

> Children don't try to be important to Jesus. And that's exactly why he welcomes them. To be near to God you cannot bring anything to impress him or to make you special in his eyes. You are not special to God because of your obedience to him. You are special to God because of his heart toward you. The Lord loves to show mercy to those who know they need it. And children are very good at knowing their need.[3]

The question for us is, *Are we very good at knowing our need as we engage with God's word?* Do we recognize our helplessness, that even our very desires need to be changed by the Spirit's transforming grace? Or do we approach Scripture pridefully, thinking we've "got this," attempting to impress God, others, and even ourselves by our obedience? Are we fairly certain we can get what we're seeking through enough well-concerted effort?

3   Jeremy Pierre, *God with Us: A Journey Home* (Wapwallopen, PA: Shepherd Press, 2021), 190.

For too many years, this was the way I approached Scripture, because I didn't understand my neediness. I thought that by opening my Bible I was seeking something good and right to do, rather than primarily seeking someone to love.

The reality is, unless we humble ourselves like little children before the Lord's word, admitting our helplessness to love what God loves and see what he sees in its pages, we will struggle to love, and we will struggle to see. The Bible will become a means to our own ends—self-righteousness, for example (John 5:44)—rather than a means of grace into satisfied hunger in God—true righteousness (Matt. 5:6).

But humility is the pathway to satisfied hunger, for it confesses its inability to find satisfaction anywhere else but in God. And our merciful God promises to answer the cry of the humble, helpless heart:

> But this is the one to whom I will look:
>> he who is humble and contrite in spirit
>> and trembles at my word. (Isa. 66:2)

Jesus, Our Great High (and Humble) Priest

When you read Isaiah 66:2, does it make you think of anyone in particular?

Only one perfectly humble heart has ever walked this earth. If the Word-made-flesh had not come to us, we would not be able to come to God. But he did. And only one perfectly humble heart is able to bring you to God as you plead with him, even now.

I think we all, as finite humans, wonder at times if our prayers are bouncing off the ceiling. But Jesus is the answer to our wondering. He is the reason our pleading prayers before God are heard, for he has become the way for us to draw near to our Father again (John 6:37; Heb. 10:20). He is our great high and humble priest. The question is, Do we actually trust that Jesus is *this eager* to help us? Do we dare believe he wants to make his joy—closeness with the Father—our joy too?

Plead for a holy hunger, friend, because Jesus has made this available to you.

As you confess your inability to want what you ought to want, imagine your great high priest saying, "I know that temptation. I fought it and overcame it so you can too" (Matt. 4:1–11). As you open his word in obedience and faith, even when you don't feel like it, remember how his perfect, righteous record of joyfully obeying and believing God's word is now yours (Rom. 3:23–25), and that he sends his Spirit to be your help, to give you spiritual insight. And as you wonder with a jaded spirit if more hunger is possible, see the Son sitting in his glory, risen from the dead, and conquering all the brokenness and sin that affects your heart (Heb. 12:1–3).

See him, and love him, and plead with God through him.

Pleading Prayers

But what exactly do we plead for?

I don't know about you, but certain things are way easier for me to pray about than others. Hunger for God and his word is one of the harder ones. I've had to ask myself why this is, and I think the answer comes back to my own helplessness.

It's easy for us to pray for what we want, but not for what we ought to want. It feels natural for us to pray for natural things, and unnatural for us to pray for spiritual things. Yet we are desperate for God to produce these very desires within us. We need him.

And so we pray. With humility and helplessness, we pray.

We ask him to give us what only he can, through Jesus Christ, by his Holy Spirit. We ask him for a miracle—a miracle of spiritual hunger that is cultivated through spiritual sight.

A sight of the Son.

Pleading for a Holy Hunger

Below are four prayers you can use to plead with God for a holy hunger. All of them are taken from his word.[4] I encourage you to use these as a springboard for creating your own prayers from other scriptures, or simply to pray them until you really *pray* them.

From Psalm 119

> O Lord, I am like a lost sheep, often going astray from you. Seek me, Lord! Call me back to your side (119:176). I do not want to forget your commandments, and I need you to incline my heart to them (119:36). It is easy for me to look at worthless things that cannot compare to you, and even prefer them. Turn my eyes, that I may look at you in your word and find life (119:37). Change my affections, that

---

4 It is generally a good principle to pray Scripture. We know that God hears us when we ask according to his will (John 14:14), and the whole Bible is his will clearly revealed to us. Two great books I recommend on biblical prayer are *Praying the Bible* by Donald S. Whitney (Wheaton, IL: Crossway, 2015) and *When Prayer Is a Struggle* by Kevin Halloran (Phillipsburg, NJ: P&R, 2021).

my deepest treasuring would be in you each day (119:72). Oh, that my ways may be steadfast in keeping your statutes (119:5)! Unless you deal well with me, Lord, I cannot keep your word, nor can I love you (119:17). Please help me choose the way of faithfulness, even when it's hard (119:30). I will run in the way of your commandments when you enlarge my heart (119:32). You have to do it, Lord! Be gracious to me according to your promise (119:58), and I know that all of your promises are Yes and Amen in your Son. In his name, amen.

From Daniel 9

O Lord, you are the great and awesome God, who keeps covenant and steadfast love with those who love you and keep your commandments. In many ways regarding your word, I have sinned and done wrong, turning aside from your commandments (9:4–6). I have often not listened to you and refused to obey your voice (9:14). You are righteous in all your ways, and I do not deserve mercy, but I am asking you to give it, according to your faithfulness. I do not present my plea before you because of my righteousness, but because of your great mercy (9:18), put on display through Jesus Christ. Make me attentive to your word. Help me listen to you and give ear to your voice. I know that refusing to listen means death to me (9:11), but I choose life. I choose Jesus. I entreat your favor and run to your truth (9:13); your word is truth. O Lord, hear; O Lord, forgive. O Lord, pay attention and act in my heart (9:19). For Jesus's glory, amen.

From Ephesians 1 and 3

Father of glory, would you please give me the Spirit of wisdom and of revelation in the knowledge of you (1:17)? Enlighten the eyes of my heart. I can't see beautiful things in your word unless you help me see (1:18). I want to know the hope to which you have called me, and the riches of my glorious inheritance in the saints. Fill me with the immeasurable greatness of your power (1:18–19), the same power that raised Jesus from the dead (1:20). Grant me to be strengthened with power through your Spirit in my inner being, so that Christ may dwell in my heart through faith as I encounter him in your word. Root and ground me in his love so I would have strength to comprehend what is the breadth and length and height and depth, and to know the love of Christ that surpasses knowledge, that I may be filled with all of your fullness, O my God (3:16–19). Amen.

From John 17

Jesus, thank you that you are mine and I am yours. Be glorified in me (17:10). Guard me and keep me in your name, and use your word to do this (17:12). Your word is a gift to me (17:14), and you have spoken so that all your people may have your joy fulfilled in us (17:13). I want more and more of your joy! Sanctify me in the truth; your word is truth (17:17). Send me into the world as an ambassador of your word. You came for this reason, Lord Jesus, that I would also be sanctified in truth and used for your glory (17:17–19). May others see in me the love that you share with your Father (17:23). I long to know you more, so please continue to make yourself known to me through your word, that I may walk by your Spirit and live in your love (17:26). In your Son's name, amen.

Hungry to Be Hungry Again

Josh (thirties, husband, father, and pastor)

For many years, I've been a leader in the church. In middle and high school, I regularly led worship and sought to study God's word with my peers. In college, I was glad to lead Bible studies on campus and serve students in a local church. And for the past ten years, I've been a pastor whose joy it is to love God's people and preach his word.

When I was in seminary, however, there was a season when I simply didn't desire the Bible. I wasn't eager to read it. I wasn't excited to study it. I had no delight in it. I had lost my appetite for it.

Which was quite alarming. I was studying to be a pastor! How could I hope to lead people *with* the Bible if I was myself apathetic *toward* it? I felt like a hypocrite, but I didn't know what to do. I knew that I should delight in God's word, that it was good to have a hunger for it, but my heart just wasn't coming along.

So what did I do? I decided that I was going to read my Bible anyway. I didn't feel like reading it, but I knew that my Christian life would shrivel up and die without it, and that I would be forfeiting the blessing of God if I continued to neglect it.

So I dragged my heart along and prayed that the Lord would help me grow to love his word. And do you know what I noticed? Over time, my heart didn't have to be dragged anymore. As I forced myself to dutifully read it (and that is how it felt!), I found myself beginning to delight in it, to crave it.

God's word created a hunger for itself.

As I committed to read and study my Bible, my appetite for it returned. Before long, I began to enjoy it and delight in it again. The truth of Psalm 1 has been my reality: there is blessing for those who delight in the law of the LORD and meditate on it day and night (Ps. 1:1–2).

[God] has spoken to us by his Son.

HEBREWS 1:2

*The Word of Christ is the instrument of Christ, used
by the Spirit of Christ, to nurture union with Christ
and to transform us into the image of Christ.*

SINCLAIR B. FERGUSON
Lessons from the Upper Room

*These things I have spoken to you, that my joy
may be in you, and that your joy may be full.*

JOHN 15:11

3

Don't Miss Jesus

HOW COULD THEY not have known?

Cleopas lay his head down, rehearsing the events of the afternoon. The stranger. His mysterious appearance. His interest in their conversation, and the intensity with which he talked about the Christ. How their hearts had burned within them when he spoke and opened to them the Scriptures.

Jesus had stood right in front of them—Jesus!—but they did not realize it.

Until he opened their eyes.

And he had used the holy Scriptures to do it. *How could they not have known?* Everywhere, throughout all the Law and the Prophets, were predictions of his suffering and foretastes of his glory. But they could not see.

Until Jesus gave them sight.

And when he did—oh, when he did!—the sight was beautiful, resonating with the burning desire deep within their hearts for God to make good on every word he had said. And he sent the Word to prove it. The Word made flesh, before their eyes.

Jesus was alive. And for them, this was only the beginning of sight.

A Sight of the Son

At this point in our time together, we have examined our hungry hearts and remembered together the necessary place of helplessness and humility before God. When it comes to loving the word, friends, we are desperate for change and for the one who alone can produce it. We long to increasingly become people who hunger for God and all he says. We want our appetites for him to grow! And so we are asking him for a miracle—a miracle of spiritual hunger that is cultivated through spiritual sight.

A sight of the Son.

This miracle is precisely what happened within two of Jesus's disciples in Luke 24.

There we read that two people were traveling together from Jerusalem to Emmaus, recounting the recent events of Jesus's torture, crucifixion, and death. While they were talking, Jesus drew near—but they didn't recognize him. He asked them what they were talking about, and with surprised and sad faces, they questioned how he could not know. So they told him the whole story.

In response, Jesus said to them,

"O foolish ones, and slow of heart to believe all that the prophets have spoken! Was it not necessary that the Christ should suffer these things and enter into his glory?" And beginning with Moses and all the Prophets, he interpreted to them in all the Scriptures the things concerning himself. (Luke 24:25–27)

In all the Scriptures. Jesus showed the disciples the wonder of his word to reveal everything necessary about himself. *The whole Bible points to Jesus, for he is the point of the whole Bible.*

Have you heard something like this before?

My guess is that you have, and that you most likely believe it. That's wonderful. So in this chapter I want to move us toward a greater desire to *encounter Jesus* as we engage with Scripture. We'll look at some principles for pursuing this end, as well as some temptations that might keep us from it.

He is the bread of life. In him, we are nourished, but without him, we wither.

And if we miss Jesus, we miss the whole point.

The Ultimate Point

So let's start right there: *What is the whole point of reading the Bible?* Is it to learn? Grow? Obey? I once asked this question to a smattering of people, and the responses were mostly encouraging. Many said they read God's word to know God. This is a great answer that reflects God's heart for us: "Hear, O Israel: The Lord our God, the Lord is one. You shall love the Lord your God with all your heart and with all your soul and with all your might." How do we do this? "And these words that I command you today shall be on your heart" (Deut. 6:4–6).

If we love the Lord, then we will take his words to heart.

We know this. We read and hear God's words in order to know the one who speaks them. But perhaps the more probing question is this: How have you seen unbelief affect this pursuit? In other words, how have you been like the disciples on the road to Emmaus, surrounded by realities *about* Jesus while remaining unaffected in heart *by* Jesus?

We can sometimes forget that Jesus is a real, risen, and reigning person, not just a spiritual theory or historical figure. We can find it more natural to look at his work than seek after his heart.

The point of our Scripture intake, then, isn't to complete a process, attain a proficiency, or fix our problems, but to meet an actual person—truly, *to encounter the risen Christ.* Only then, as we encounter Jesus, will our appetite for him grow.

Two Temptations (and Two Opportunities)

All of us come from different backgrounds, cultures, and families, as well as beliefs and habits as they relate to the Bible. For the sake of time, I want to focus on two specific temptations we can face, as well as two opportunities, related to opening our Bibles and encountering Jesus there. We'll call the temptations "foolishness" and "slowness of heart," following Jesus's words in Luke 24.

Foolishness (and Wisdom)

Foolishness and wisdom are two opposing themes woven throughout the Bible, and the book of Proverbs relates them to God's words: "For the LORD gives wisdom; / from his mouth come knowledge and understanding" (Prov. 2:6).

The fool forsakes God's counsel and teaching, turns to his own devices, and loves worldly gain, to his demise (see Prov. 1:24–33). He lacks right judgment and good sense. But the wise person hears Wisdom's call and responds to her:

> How long, O simple ones, will you love being simple?
> How long will scoffers delight in their scoffing
>   and fools hate knowledge?
> If you turn at my reproof,
> behold, I will pour out my spirit to you;
>   I will make my words known to you. (Prov. 1:22–23)

If foolishness means lacking right judgment, then we are often tempted to be foolish as it relates to Scripture. We have the words of life at our fingertips, the very voice of Jesus—but to us, it can be dull and boring, a task to be checked off our list. We have an invitation from God to "come to the waters," to draw from the one who is full of grace and truth—but we suspect that this invitation must be for other people, or that it must come with a slight reluctancy or mild disapproving gaze. (God can't be *that* inviting . . . can he?) We have a God of perfect sufficiency to meet our every need, and we know, deep down, that we are needy—but we would rather supply for ourselves, thank you very much.

Our human tendency toward foolishness means our thoughts of God are terribly skewed. Which means our thinking about his word is, too.

God's word feels boring and familiar to us, so we turn to shiny entertainment, putting off eternal things until a more pressing time. The Bible seems too demanding or confusing, so we walk away from it, perpetually discouraged. Its words seem insufficient and sometimes irrelevant, so we look elsewhere to hear from Jesus. We fear falling into a legalistic mindset about God's word, so we major on grace and minor on obedience.

Our foolishness tempts us to forget what Scripture is and forgo its blessings.

But as we consider what it means to encounter Jesus in his word, we can rejoice instead that "the Bible is help, not oppression. . . . Our own dark thoughts of God are what cause us to shrink back from opening and yielding to it."[1] What if, rather than shrinking back, we receive Wisdom's call, realizing that God *wants* to make his words known to us? What if, instead of distrusting God, we distrust ourselves? What if we increasingly turn away from foolishness because we recognize that it produces within us a slowness of heart to believe Jesus?

Slowness of Heart (and Hunger)

The second temptation we often face is unbelief, or what Jesus calls *slowness of heart.* Jesus once said to the religious leaders, men who were thoroughly versed in Scripture,

> [The Father's] voice you have never heard, his form you have never seen, and you do not have his word abiding in you, *for you do not believe the one whom he has sent.* You search the Scriptures because you think that in them you have eternal

1 Dane Ortlund, *Deeper: Real Change for Real Sinners* (Wheaton, IL: Crossway, 2021), 148.

life; and it is they that bear witness about me, yet *you refuse to come to me that you may have life*. (John 5:37–40)

Jesus is addressing the heart behind their habits. It is possible to search the Scriptures and miss its main character. It is possible to give the Bible our attention, but not to give Jesus our affection—our whole hearts.

It is possible to come to the word, but not to come to the Word.

Personally, this is my main temptation. I can wrongly believe that my reading and study habits earn God's approval, rather than enjoying his approval through these habits. I can read, read, read until my eyeballs fall out, but if that reading isn't followed by a change of heart that hungers for Jesus more, then I have not truly come to him. I can search the Scriptures, but if this doesn't lead to seeking *him* as a person, then I have not actually come to him.

If I may dare say it, I wonder if many believers today who have been trained in their homes and churches to study the Bible are at risk of becoming like the religious leaders of Jesus's time: scholars of the word, but strangers to the Word. One of my greatest concerns is that Jesus would say to me, "Depart from me, I never knew you"—even though I had been a vigorous student of Scripture.

Oh Lord, may your precious word quicken our slow hearts and stir our hunger for you! May we seek you in all of Scripture, and come to you for life.

Just as the disciples on the road to Emmaus were able to recount all the things that had happened *to* Jesus, they were still not able to see *him*. And he was right in front of them the whole time. Oh, that we would not miss Jesus! For if we miss him, we miss life itself.

We miss the very life to whom all of Scripture bears witness, and for whom we were made to hunger.

Don't Miss Jesus

The obvious follow-up question, then, is, *How do we not miss Jesus?*

How do we fight foolishness and unbelief, pursuing wisdom and a quickened, hungry heart for God as we open his word? There is no magic bullet here, only a constant dependence on God's supernatural help as we put ourselves in the position to receive from him. Following are a few biblical principles by which we might do this, and I'm praying the Lord will use these in our hearts to grow our affection for the word of Christ.

Call upon the Spirit of Christ

How exactly does God intervene in our hearts as we depend on him? He does this through his Holy Spirit, who opens blind eyes and gives us a spiritual sight of the Son (2 Cor. 3:17–18). The Spirit's role is to glorify Jesus (John 16:14), and he makes Jesus more beautiful to our hearts as we read and hear his word. This is why he is called the Spirit of truth. He is the very spirit of Christ, given to us for our help (John 14:16–17, 26). He is such a special person that Jesus said it would actually be *better* if he went away and the Spirit came (John 16:7)!

We need the Spirit to reveal Christ to us in the whole Bible, to debunk false conceptions of him, and to replace our doubts with truth about God's character and heart. We need him to help us think God's thoughts after him. So we "[make our ears] attentive" to him; we "call out for insight and raise [our] voice for understanding"; we "seek it like silver and search for it as for hidden treasures," believing that, as God pours out his Spirit to us (Prov. 2:1–5), we will "understand the fear of the LORD and find the knowledge of God" (Prov. 2:5). We call upon the Spirit of Jesus so we do not miss Jesus.

Dig into the Words of Christ

As we have touched on before, we cannot know Jesus without knowing his word. But our concern about heartless forms of Bible reading and study shouldn't keep us from digging into it. Instead, it is good and wise that we would be wary of unbelief as we open God's word; this will act as a guardrail against temptation and spur us on toward our ultimate goal, which is to encounter and love the risen Jesus.

Because God's word *is* God's words, the more we pursue taking his words to heart, the better we will know him and the more we will love him (John 15:9–10). So how might you get more of God's words into your soul? How might you dig deeper into specific texts? Or read more widely across the whole Bible? What books or other resources could you read or listen to, created by those who have studied Scripture? We'll venture into more of these ideas in chapter 6.[2]

---

2 Appendix 2 lists books that will help you trust, approach, read, and study your Bible.

God's word is a treasure that we will never exhaust (Ps. 19:10; Prov. 2:4), and every sight of Jesus is only a beginning. So let's dig into the Bible. There is so much more of him to behold in its pages (Rom. 11:33; Eph. 3:8).

Lean upon the Body of Christ

I have asked my husband and my sisters in Christ to pray for my heart as it relates to God and his word so many times—when the seed feels like it's falling on hard ground, when my affections lie dormant, when I've desired other glories and pursuits over Jesus. So I have asked my church family to help me process the slowness of heart I'm experiencing (Prov. 20:5), to pray for me (James 5:16), and to speak over me the truth about God when he feels far away (2 Cor. 1:3–4). I have sat under the ministry of the preached word and been fed when I have struggled to feed myself (Col. 3:15–17).

The body of Christ has been just that to me: *his body* (1 Cor. 12:12). His gentle hands and intentional feet. His comforting presence. His compassionate gaze. His sure and steady voice.

You too, friend, can call upon the body of Christ in your time of need. We seek him together, and we show him to one another. This is why the local church is such a vital part of the health of our souls, and such a privilege to be part of.

This leads to my next encouragement: the Bibles in your church and the Bibles in your home are privileges—gifts from God's hand—that we often take for granted. His word is a gift to be received and hungered for and enjoyed.

Encountering Jesus

1. Which of the two temptations do you most relate to? Using the Temptation Lies and Truths table, identify lies associated with each of these in your own heart, and then replace those lies with truth.

Temptations, Lies, and Truths

Temptations	Lie(s)	Truth(s)
Foolishness: skewed thoughts of God and his word that affect our pursuit of him	E.g., "The Bible is boring."	
Slowness of Heart: unbelief that leads us to give the Bible our attention, but not to give Jesus our affection	E.g., "God is disappointed in me."	

2. Read the opening story from Luke 24:13–35, and envision yourself as one of the disciples. What would it have been like to finally realize that you had been with Jesus all along? How does this change the way you might pray for the Spirit's help in seeing him?

3. Professor and author Kelly Kapic writes that we all have "preconceptions of God informed by unbiblical impulses." He encourages us to "take careful note of the places that the Bible's descriptions of God make us uncomfortable, and ask why they do so. These observations," he says, "reveal broader problems in our thinking and attitudes. These are the places to dig in and rebuild."[3] The next time you come to one of these places in your Bible reading, take note, ask why, and dig in.

4. The next time you read your Bible (or hear a sermon), try using these five questions to look for Jesus in the passage you're reading:

    a. Is there a promise that Jesus has fulfilled, or will fulfill?

    b. Is there a terrible person that Jesus is the opposite of? Or a wonderful person that Jesus is the perfect version of?[4]

    c. Is there a command that Jesus has fully obeyed?

    d. Is there a sin, pattern of sin, conflict, or problem that Jesus has conquered?

    e. Is there a need, longing, or hunger that only Jesus can meet?

---

3 Kelly M. Kapic, *Embodied Hope: A Theological Meditation on Pain and Suffering* (Downers Grove, IL: IVP Academic, 2017), 12.

4 This is called *typology*, where figures in the Bible are "types" of the Christ to come.

A Treasury of the Lord's Compassion

Aubrey (thirties, single, fundraising consultant, youth group leader)

In my midtwenties I walked through a year of deep anxiety following a stressful dating relationship. My mind felt constantly assaulted with thoughts I couldn't control—accusation of sin, fear that something horrible would happen to me or because of me, and exhaustion from trying to stay focused. Most nights I barely slept.

This anxiety was quickly joined by doubts over my salvation. I imagined God as stingy and punitive, and maybe not real. I couldn't read some parts of Scripture, especially Jesus's sermons, because he seemed too angry. God seemed to reserve his love and salvation for those who followed him perfectly, which I knew I was not doing. I had to stop reading the Bible too close to bedtime because my mind would fixate on a harsh-sounding verse and turn it over all night long.

But the Lord gave me friends who were constant and firm in reminding me of what was true. An older friend spoke Scripture to me every time we met, and she encouraged me to safeguard my time in God's word. At first I read the same few psalms over and over. I read psalms where the writer praised God for saving him in a time of distress, for being a refuge, and for never forsaking his saints. In these psalms, God wasn't stingy; he was a rescuer.

I read the last few chapters of Job, where God lays out his consistent, loving care for all the creatures of the earth. I read a scene in Zechariah 3 where Satan accuses the high priest before the Lord, but God defends him as his own chosen one and declares him forgiven and clean.

I tentatively started reading the Gospels again—and to my relief I saw that Jesus's ministry was full of healing, casting out demons, and seeking out people who needed him. Even his hard teachings were driving toward an invitation to come to him and receive true life.

Over that year, I learned to see Scripture as a treasury of the Lord's compassion. In my anxious season, he showed me what was true about him. And in the years since, I have been grateful time and time again that he taught me that his word is the place to seek and find these truths.

Did any people ever hear the voice of a god speaking out of the midst of the fire, as you have heard, and still live?

DEUTERONOMY 4:33

Long ago, at many times and in many ways, God spoke to our fathers by the prophets, but in these last days he has spoken to us by his Son.

HEBREWS 1:1–2

God [has made] his mind known to sinners.

J. I. PACKER
A Quest for Godliness

4

Remember the Privilege

IF YOU ARE READING THIS, you can thank God for Johannes Gutenberg.

Though Gutenberg wasn't the first inventor of a printing press, his version was the first to be easily replicated and therefore widespread, advancing the literary world as we know it. Before the German inventor had ever tinkered with metal, ink, and paper, producing that magical combination of printed glory we call publishing, few individuals and families owned books—including Bibles.

Friends, if that Bible on your coffee table or bookshelf had existed five hundred years ago, you would have been the anomaly—rich in resources and utterly privileged.

The reality today? *You still are.*

As we struggle with the desire to love God's word, we will be greatly helped to remember what a gift it is, both in its nature and its prevalence. After talking to many people over the years, it seems to me that one of our modern hindrances to loving and hungering for God's word is that it has become boring to us.

The Bible is so ubiquitous, and our Western Christian pursuit of its knowledge so wonderfully common, that we forget how precious it truly is. We forget that we don't deserve such a gift.

And so, we will do well *to remember*.

In this chapter, to encourage our hearts toward a greater hunger for God and his precious words, I want us to remember. Specifically, I want us to rehearse and freshly count three privileges we often take for granted as they relate to our Bibles: revelation, resources, and religious freedom. (We could cover many more, I'm sure!) In doing so, I am praying that the Lord will stir within us a deep and renewed gratitude for the abundance he has lavished upon us in the form of a book—a book that, with cover, pages, and printed words, holds the very voice of God.

The Privilege of Revelation

Have you ever wondered what it would be like if God had not spoken? I realize this question presents some immediate problems. (For example, there could not be a world without God speaking it into being [Gen. 1].) But set these problems aside for a moment and envision how our world might be different if God had never communicated with us.

A Famine of Words

Let's start by considering Israel's history. One of its darkest periods was the four hundred years when God stopped speaking to his people. In Kevin DeYoung's estimation, "There is no calamity like the silence of God."[1] To be without the

---

1   Kevin DeYoung, *Taking God At His Word: Why the Bible Is Knowable, Necessary, and Enough, and What That Means for You and Me* (Wheaton, IL: Crossway, 2016), 21.

gracious voice of our Creator is perhaps one of the greatest tragedies we could know. So when God's people continued to rebel against him, after he had extended his mercy to them time and again, after he had performed miraculous wonders on their behalf, and after he had patiently provided for their every need, God spoke of an upcoming day of deep darkness—the turning away of his face and the silence of his mouth:

> "Behold, the days are coming," declares the Lord GOD,
>   "when I will send a famine on the land—
> not a famine of bread, nor a thirst for water,
>   but of hearing the words of the LORD.
> They shall wander from sea to sea,
>   and from north to east;
> they shall run to and fro, to seek the word of the LORD,
>   but they shall not find it." (Amos 8:11–12)

About three hundred years after Amos's prophecy, God's people would experience divine starvation. His word about his words would prove true: God ceased speaking to his people. No communication. No merciful warnings. No gracious instruction. No sense of his presence. Instead, *silence*, brought about by the people's disdain for God's words. Only exile, turmoil, confusion, and destruction. Only calamity.

So when God warns his people that a famine is on the horizon, a famine "of hearing the words of the LORD," it's hard to imagine being in their shoes. But for a moment, let's try.

What might *our* world look like if God had not spoken, or if he stopped speaking? Think of the calamity. Evil would be multiplied, and wickedness rampant. The love of self and the inward quest for "truth" would speed along with flying colors, leaving neighbor-love and any sense of universal morality in the dust. We would be on our own—a frightening position to be in—and given up to the ramifications of our twisted human folly.

We would be left hungry for truth. Hungry for hope. Hungry for transcendence. We would be left searching for faith in something stronger than us, hoping against hope in something more lasting than us and pining for love from someone more trustworthy than us. And every quest would prove elusive, unearthing only disappointment and emptiness. *Calamity.*

We would be utterly without God in an aimless and hopeless world (Eph. 2:12).

The Giving of the Word

The good news? *This is not our reality.*

Our God, who isn't obligated to speak to sinners, *has spoken and is speaking to us.* What a privilege! We live in a world saturated with the voice of God, in a testifying creation that declares his goodness and power whether we acknowledge this or not (Pss. 19:1–2; 29:3; Rom. 1:18–20). Despite the world's darkness and chaos, the heavens shout his glory. Despite its many evils and sufferings, the skies sing of his praise.

And into this world, God himself came.

Jesus, the Son—the fullness of God, the image of God, and the Word of God—clothed himself in flesh to reveal

God to us. The bread of life came to satisfy our hunger for truth, hope, and transcendence, to be the author and perfecter of our faith, the sure and steadfast anchor of our hopeful souls, and love incarnate, with arms spread wide on a cross to prove it. In the calamity of our starving hunger, God didn't leave us to ourselves but met us with his perfect Word—his own Son.

Then, to tell us all there is to know about Jesus, he gives us the written word. God graciously breaks into the world of undeserving, hungry people like you and me—the divine and holy One reaching down to us and offering us himself—through the Bible. *Revealing. Communicating. Speaking.* Shining light into our hearts so we can see.

This encourages us and gives us perspective: *the Bible is anything but boring.*

So, the next time you are tempted to think low and mundane thoughts of your Bible (which all of us probably do at some point), consider that God never had to speak to you in the first place but has chosen to reveal his Son there, opening his holy mouth for your faith, hope, and joy in Jesus Christ. Consider the Israelites, gone before you, who sought God's word but could not find it. Consider that the book for which you struggle to hunger is no ordinary book, but contains the mind of Almighty God whose powerful and divine utterance, which should obliterate us (Deut. 4:33; Heb. 12:18–19), has been graciously wrapped in accessible human words on paper pages, printed with ink.

Consider what a privilege it is to hold in your hands the very revelation of God, and worship the Word whom it reveals.

The Privilege of Resources

Now consider that Bibles no longer cost an annual salary.

Today, we can buy a Bible for about an hour's wage. We can take one for free from the hotel nightstand. We can download a Bible onto our phones. But centuries ago, before Gutenberg's world-changing invention, a hand-copied Bible would have cost a year's worth of pay.[2] Because of the high expense, few individuals and families owned Bibles, and instead they depended on oral tradition to know and understand Scripture. Added to this was the common person's low literacy rate and inability to read Latin, the most prevalent biblical language before vernacular translations appeared.

What does all this have to do with us today?

Our present-day experience of owning multiple copies, translations, and versions of the Bible (or having easy, immediate access to them) is historically unmatched. Five hundred years ago Bibles were rare—and what is rare is deemed precious.

Have you ever considered that our lack of hunger for Scripture might be related to a perceived loss of its preciousness? With the advent of Gutenberg's printing press, Bibles (and other books) became more widely available to families, making literacy more desirable and attainable for common people. Now, the majority of us don't think twice about our ability to access, read, and understand literature, including Scripture.

Think about it. Need a different version of a Bible verse? You can find it for free online. Are you confused about what a pas-

2   "How Was the Bible Distributed before the Printing Press Was Invented in 1455?," *Biblica*, https://www.biblica.com/. Accessed July 2022.

sage means? Just pull out your study Bible and read the notes. Didn't get to your reading plan this morning? Turn on your audio Bible in the car and listen while you drive. We do all of these actions as literate people with millions of resources at our fingertips. Amazing! What a wonderful gift it is to live in the twenty-first century, when it seems we lack for nothing in the world of biblical assets. *Our great opportunity is to prize what has become pervasive, and to not lose sight of its infinite preciousness.*

The word of God is "more to be desired than even much fine gold" (Ps. 19:10). God, in his manifold power and wisdom, has seen fit to preserve his words throughout the ages for our salvation and for our satisfaction in him; and as we recognize how extraordinary this is, we will hunger for the words he has preserved and multiplied, and for the one who speaks them.

We will count it a great privilege to open his divine book and seek him in it.[3]

The Privilege of Religious Freedom

In the early twentieth century, a Korean believer named Ahn Ei Sook (also known as Esther Ahn Kim) was preparing herself for imprisonment. The Japanese government had annexed Korea, forcing its people to worship their gods under threat of punishment—and Ei Sook resolved that she would not bow to any god but the Lord Jesus. In preparation for her inevitable jail time, the young woman committed hundreds of Scripture

---

3 One of the best talks I have heard on the extraordinary nature of the Bible is Steven Lawson's message "Is the Bible Just Another Book?" which he gave at Ligonier's 2010 National Conference. Please listen to it; you won't be disappointed: https://www .youtube.com/.

passages to memory. She knew her precious Bible would be confiscated, and that her soul depended on storing up God's word in her heart.[4]

We would like to believe that Ei Sook's story is a thing of the past, but it's not. Today, around the globe, Christians are persecuted for their faith, church attendance is a crime, and Bible ownership is equally punishable by law. Those of us who live in countries where we know the privilege of religious freedom might find it hard to imagine such an existence, but it's beneficial to try.

Imagine that today will be the last day you can read a Bible for decades. Does this cause you to think differently about it? How might this change your hunger for God's words?

Imagine that your church has been shut down, and that you won't hear Bible preaching for the foreseeable future. Would you feel its loss? Would this make a difference to your soul?

The reality that we can still freely access, own, open, hear, read, understand, and share Scripture—the very voice of God illuminating our dark world and satisfying starving souls—is a pure gift that we will do well to treasure. Who knows if there will be a day when our Western freedoms change and we end up in Ei Sook's position? Will we consider God's word a precious treasure to be sought, daily bread to be eaten, living water to be consumed?

Will we hunger for it as the great privilege it is?

---

4   Catherine Parks, *12 Faithful Women: Portraits of Steadfast Endurance*, eds. Kristen Wetherell and Melissa Kruger (The Gospel Coalition, 2020), 19–32.

May our answer be *yes, Lord*, and may we feast on the abundance of God's words both individually and alongside our church family.

That is where we will turn in the next chapter.

Remembering the Privilege

1. Read Psalm 81. Write down in the table below every instance of God's pleading with his people to listen to him and take his voice seriously. (I have provided some verses for you.)

   Then consider the following questions in response: How would you describe the yearning of God's heart for his people? What is his desire for them? Do you hear him pleading the same things for you today?

   Psalm 81

Verse 8
Verse 10

Verse 11

Verse 12

Verse 13

Verse 14

Verse 15

2. Let's revisit the imaginary scenarios under the religious freedom
   section. Write down your reactions and responses.

   Scenario 1: Imagine that today is your last day to read the
      Bible for decades. How does this cause you to think
      differently about it? How might this change your hunger
      for God's words?

   Scenario 2: Imagine that your church has been shut down
      and that you won't hear Bible preaching for the foresee-
      able future. Will you feel its loss? How so? How might
      the absence of preaching make a difference to your soul?

3. Read biographies of Christians from other parts of the world (such
   as the Gospel Coalition's *12 Faithful Women: Portraits of Steadfast
   Endurance* and *12 Faithful Men: Portraits of Courageous Endurance
   in Pastoral Ministry*). These can give perspective and foster a fresh
   appreciation for the freedoms and resources we enjoy.

> **Reviving the Soul, Rejoicing the Heart**
>
> *Davis (twenties, husband, father,
> copyeditor, and deacon)*
>
> From my teen years to my midtwenties, I can truly say
> I loved the Bible. I found the stories to be epic, and
> they awakened my imagination and produced awe for
> God's character. The poetry brought inspiration, cre-
> ativity, and bursts of theological insight. The teachings

motivated me toward Christlikeness and illuminated the world around me.

Based on my description above, you might get the impression that I had no room to grow in my love of God's word. That's what I thought; God knew otherwise! Hindsight tells me that while I loved and listened to the Bible, I also loved and listened to other books and teachings, placing them in same category of influence as God's word.

Don't get me wrong; I am not against other books! But I had set them up in the high places of my heart. This led me to evaluate the Bible by their standards and expressions, and it produced in me a lingering doubt over whether the Bible always said things in the right way. Doing so also turned the Bible into one option among many, as if the choice between Genesis and Gilgamesh was simply the choice between cookie dough and chocolate ice cream.

Then Psalm 19 walked into my life. Or maybe it burst into my world! As I read the first verse ("The heavens declare the glory of God, / and the sky above proclaims his handiwork"), the thought of God's sovereignty, his work as Creator, his efforts to speak to me, and his great glory all hit me and overwhelmed me. And then, as if for the first time, when I read verse 7 ("The law of the LORD is perfect, / reviving the soul"), a craving was produced in me—right then and there. All of a sudden, I wanted that revival for my soul. I saw myself as simple, and I wanted to be wise. I wanted my heart to rejoice. I needed God's word like never before.

Jesus talked about a man who scattered some seeds, which sprouted and produced fruit without the man knowing how to explain it (Mark 4:26–29). This is similar to my story. I do not know how to explain what happened; I just know that it did. On one regular weekday morning, God used Psalm 19 to make alive within me a joy that had once been dead.

*[The children of mankind] feast on the abundance of your
house,
and you give them drink from the river of your delights.*

PSALM 36:8

*The Word of God is meant to be a community
treasure and a community event.*

JOHN PIPER
When I Don't Desire God

*Devote yourself to the public reading of Scripture,
to exhortation, to teaching. . . . for by so doing
you will save both yourself and your hearers.*

1 TIMOTHY 4:13, 16

5

Feast with Your Church

"IT FEELS LIKE it's something I'm *supposed* to do."

Heads nodded in agreement. Our small group was talking about reading our Bibles in the season of early parenthood with little kids needing us all the time. The phrase "supposed to" popped up more than once, and the universal struggle was evident.

These women *wanted* to want to read their Bibles. But it didn't always happen.

Does that sound familiar to you?

This is a common reality for hungry believers with full lives. We know that reading Scripture is good for us—we know we're "supposed to"—but when the choice to read doesn't come with feelings of enjoyment, or when we end up choosing other things, we sink down into guilt. And the deep hole of guilt can be hard to climb out of.

Only later did the irony of our conversation occur to me: these believers, who were lamenting how hard it is to engage with Scripture, were doing just that. Right then. *Together.* These women regularly attended Sunday worship services with their families and were involved in a word-centric small group. *They were feeding on God's word with God's people.* And this reality changes things.

It's the kind of encouragement that will help us climb out from the guilt hole.

Pietism and False Guilt

Where does this sense of guilt come from?

You know the thoughts: *I should want to read my Bible. I should be reading my Bible more often. I should be getting more out of it.* And while some of these considerations can be good and helpful, awakening us to obstacles and our tendency to hunger for things other than God, many are often rooted in false guilt.

In other words, we can feel bad about our engagement with Scripture, but we might have no God-given reason to. *Our guilt may be false because there is no command in the Bible about having a daily quiet time.*[1]

---

1 Yes, there are commands about loving the Lord with all our heart, soul, mind, and strength (Mark 12:30). There are commands to keep in step with the Spirit, who teaches us the truth about the gospel through Scripture (Gal. 5:1–26). And there are commands to hold fast to the word of life, to not be deceived by false teaching, and to hold our original confidence firm to the very end (Phil. 2:16; 1 Tim. 4:6–16; Heb. 3:14). But is there any command like "you shall arise at five in the morning, coffee in hand, and spend time with the Lord alone for two hours"? No. And if we are honest, this is usually what we think about when we feel bad about not reading the word like we're "supposed to." But God isn't prescriptive about this in his word. Instead, he commands proper priorities for the growth of our souls in him: "But seek first the kingdom of God and his righteousness, and [everything else you need] will be added to you" (Matt. 6:33). He wants us to hunger for the bread of life, not for an idealistic formula. He wants us to pursue the Word, not a perfect quiet time (as if there were such a thing).

So where did this idea of "quiet time" come from, anyway? It came from a movement that has impacted the way we interact with God's word, which we know as the Pietistic Movement.

Pietism was spearheaded in the seventeenth century by German Protestants whose main goal was to promote individual Christian experience. After centuries of dependence on Roman Catholic priests to hear and understand the Bible, Pietists envisioned believers walking with God personally, growing in holiness and knowledge of God's word themselves. This is one of Pietism's positive influences, along with its emphasis on our walk with Jesus. But it also unhelpfully narrowed our view of what it means to engage with the Bible.

Enter the popular Christian idea of "quiet time."

Enter the false guilt many of us feel about it.

In Western Christian culture, we assume certain components for this personal habit. Solitude. Silence. An hour or two of reading, study, meditation, and prayer. Good coffee in an inspirational mug. Perhaps some soft worship music in the background. But how realistic are these, really? (This mom is shaking her head as her kids scream in the background.)

True, as individuals, we will not grow in our hunger for God apart from *personally* knowing him and loving his word. But if we limit our engagement with Scripture to this individualized "quiet time" format—even without realizing it—we not only fall into false guilt and discouragement, but we also miss the many creative (and biblical!) ways of nourishing our souls with it—such as our main spiritual meal.

Your Main Spiritual Meal

Most Americans eat three main meals every day: breakfast, lunch, and dinner. We need these meals for proper nutrition and growth. We may be able to snack our way through the day for a while, but a sporadic, limited way of eating won't sustain or strengthen us in the long run. Whole, well-rounded meals are necessary in order for us to grow.

So, in light of the concept of "quiet time," here's a question worth pondering: Have you considered that your main spiritual meal is to be enjoyed *at church*?

When you think about engaging with your Bible, does your thinking include the weekly worship service? Does it involve consuming Scripture alongside God's people? Do you believe that this important "meal" matters? It doesn't just matter. It is the believer's *main spiritual sustenance*.

But, you may be wondering, *isn't it important for believers to be sustained, day by day, by reading their Bibles?* Of course it is! Private, devotional reading and study are very good things, as we have seen so far throughout this book. We will look at this practice more in the next chapter. But Scripture shows us that God's words have overarchingly been directed to his gathered people, not solely to individuals.

For example, when God spoke the Ten Commandments to Moses on Mount Sinai, he intended them for the Israelites, his redeemed people (Ex. 20). When God spoke to the prophets, bringing them his words of remembrance and warning, he told them to relay these words to his wayward people (Isa. 1:4; Jer. 2:1–13). When God spoke his law through prophets like Joshua (Josh. 24) and kings like Josiah (2 Kings 23:1–2) and priests like Ezra (Ezra 7:10; Neh. 8:1–3), he did so in the hearing of all God's people.

And what about the New Testament? This section of our present-day Bible was composed for the early church, God's gathered people. Whenever you read your New Testament, you are reading historical accounts leading up to the church (like the Gospels and Acts), letters to the church (like 1 and 2 Cor., Eph., and Rom.), and prophecy about the church (Rev.).

The Lord clearly loves communicating with his people as the gathered church. And this reality tells us something vital about what happens on a Sunday morning.

One Sunday Morning

I walked through the doors of our church with my kids running ahead of me, excited to find their daddy (who is the pastor). It might have been hard to get there that morning, but it was worth it. Simply the presence of other believers encouraged my weary heart. They believed church matters, which helped me believe it too. Within our many differences, we had the same destination on a Sunday morning. The same truth sustained us. The same Lord united us.

We were hungry for him together.

Once the kids were settled, I sat down next to my husband, and the worship service began. The noise of the world grew dim as the voices of the redeemed rose. God's truth stilled our busy and scattered hearts, as his light dispelled our darkness and hope anchored us to the unseen.

The primary spiritual meal of our week was set before us, and we feasted. Through a sumptuous banquet for our hungry souls, God's word nourished us. Together.

Nourished Together

This is simply a snapshot of one church on one Sunday morning. Yours probably looks different than ours; but the unifying hope is that *worship is our priority, with God's word at the center of it*, that we feast on Scripture together and are strengthened in the word of Christ for the week ahead.

The question worth asking at this point is, *Am I committed to a local church that loves the word of Christ?* No church is perfect. But if you are disconnected from church, or if your church is not consuming the Scriptures on Sunday mornings (or whenever you meet), you are missing out on the meal that matters most to your spiritual health and to the spiritual health of other believers. It is never too late to connect or make a change.[2]

That said, what exactly happens at our worship gatherings, as the primary spiritual meal of our week is set before us? Churches feast on God's word during a worship service through at least four means: singing it, praying it, reading it, and hearing it preached.

Singing God's Word

In a church service, singing songs to and about the Lord has become so normal for us that we often don't consider why

---

2   If this is your situation, you might consider using the Gospel Coalition's "Church Finder" to locate a solid, Bible-preaching church in your area: https://www.thegospel coalition.org/churches/.

we're doing it. If the "singing part" disappeared, would it really matter? According to Scripture, it would.

Singing together is a gift, a deeply spiritual practice that God uses to nourish our souls with the truth of his word. It is also a biblical command: "Let the word of Christ dwell in you richly, teaching and admonishing one another in all wisdom, *singing psalms and hymns and spiritual songs, with thankfulness in your hearts to God*" (Col. 3:16). Paul writes to the Colossian church, and he connects the indwelling of the "word of Christ" with "singing."

When we sing the word, we are letting it nourish our souls.

In singing together about Christ and his many words, promises, and works—extolling what we see of him in the Bible—we are feasting on him and satisfying our hunger for him.[3] We are encouraging our brothers and sisters, who need to hear the truth proclaimed through our voices, and they are encouraging us. We are memorizing great truths that will stay with us throughout the week (because songs are sticky!). And we are offering our collective praise to God, which brings him honor and magnifies him before the world.

We feast on God's word through the gift of corporate singing.

Praying God's Word

Another way we feast as a church family is through praying together and calling upon God according to his word. It's easy to let our minds wander during the pastoral prayer ("Did

---

3   It is worth saying that not every worship song is biblical and focused primarily on worshiping God. Many modern worship songs are more about us than him! We will be nourished if the songs we sing together are rooted in God's words, not ours.

I shut the garage door . . . ?"), but instead we stay engaged with it, praying along with our leaders in our hearts. We make their prayers our own, thankful that someone is giving voice to the congregation's needs, confessions, and praises. This is a wonderful blessing!

One of the best ways we can enjoy Scripture is by letting it shape our prayers, both individually and corporately. My senior pastor encourages us to "always pray with an open Bible." We have a treasure trove of prayers in Scripture that will direct our minds and hearts to God and his will. We don't need to wonder if we are praying rightly if we're praying straight from his word.

So, during your next worship service, receive corporate prayers as a gift and let them nourish your soul with the truth. You might even ask for a copy of the prayers, and then pray them throughout the week or use them as a guide for your own.

We feast on God's word through the gift of corporate prayer.

Reading God's Word

Scripture reading may be the most obvious way we enjoy God's word, as the Bible is opened and read over us during corporate worship. Again, what a gift this is! We have the privilege of pausing our harried and full lives to receive Scripture in the company of other believers. We have a set-apart opportunity to breathe in God's breathed-out words, to hear, and to believe.

Friend, I want to encourage you: *this matters!* Don't label the Sunday morning Scripture reading as a mere routine. Each Sunday your soul is being washed with the cleansing, life-giving words of God. Receive with thanksgiving the congregational reading of Scripture. It is part of your primary spiritual meal that will nourish you throughout the week.

We feast on God's word through the gift of corporate Scripture reading.

Hearing God's Word Preached

Long before your bleary eyes open on a Sunday morning and you stand next to your church family to worship Jesus, your pastor has put on his "chef's hat" to create a nourishing meal for you. He begins on his knees, prayerfully asking the Lord to give him the right and best ingredients. Then he diligently prepares over the next several days, studying Scripture, grasping its message, and communicating how that message applies to the church today.

He works hard for you, and the work *is* hard, but all along the way your pastor is tasting and seeing that the Lord is good (Ps. 34:8), being nourished by God in the process. It is the Lord's joy—and your pastor's—to prepare a table before you so your soul is strengthened for the week ahead (Ps. 23:5). This is what the sermon does.

So when you enter the sanctuary to worship God on a Sunday morning, a great and supernatural work has been happening behind the scenes. God is ready to serve you his word through your pastor. Be ready to receive a life-giving, carefully crafted meal—from God's mouth, through your pastor's mouth, straight to your soul.

This, too, matters. The preaching of God's word is vital to our spiritual health. So, as we hear the sermon, we stay engaged. We may take notes to follow along, chewing on what the pastor is saying, asking questions, and pleading with the Spirit to teach us. Once again, we praise God for this gift—a nourishing meal to strengthen our souls in Christ—and we receive the sermon as God's gracious words to a hungry and needy church family.

We feast on God's word through the gift of preaching.

Feast on the Abundance of God's House

The next time you feel discouraged and guilty about not reading your Bible the way you think you're "supposed to," do this instead: remember the previous Sunday at church, and breathe a sigh of relief and praise.

You *have* consumed God's word. More than that, you have feasted on its abundance.

Through singing it, praying it, reading it, and hearing it preached alongside God's gathered and beloved people, you have "let the word of Christ dwell in you richly." Your soul has been truly nourished.

And over time, your appetite for God's words will grow, and your hunger for him will be satisfied.

Feasting with Your Church

1. Think about your last worship service. (Or think about these prompts during your next one.) Naming all the ingredients of the feast will help you recognize and appreciate it more. You might even journal your way through the service so you can revisit the various Scripture passages throughout the week. In what ways did you:

- Sing the Bible?
- Pray the Bible?
- Read the Bible?
- Hear the Bible preached?

2. When you dine at a gourmet restaurant, your enjoyment of the meal both compliments the chef and also brings you delight and strength. In the greatest way, feasting on God's word in church brings honor to him, the head chef, and delight and nourishment to his people, who enjoy him. In a consumerist culture, how does this change your perspective about the purpose of church?

3. Read Psalm 73. The psalmist, Asaph, is battling spiritual depression and a lack of satisfaction in God. Verses 16–17 are the turning point. What changes his perspective and moves his heart to joy and assurance again?

The Long, Good Work of God's Word

Amanda (forties, wife, mother, and content director)

I was raised on Scripture. My parents both had minor degrees in Bible from a respectable university. For generations, my family had prayed, taught, and listened to the word of God and tried hard to live its truth. Early in life, I remember memorizing long psalms that helped us all weather the storm of a severe childhood illness that kept me house- and hospital-bound.

Given what I knew from memorization and a lifetime of osmosis, I vividly recall the shame of feeling like an imposter as a young mom when I realized that, though my faith was rock-solid, my Old Testament knowledge was . . . nil. Beyond the psalms and the flannel board Sunday school top ten, I had no depth in any Old Testament teaching.

It might stand to reason that somehow, through my own humility and determination, I managed to turn this around. But that would be far from the truth. Rather, God has been gracious and patient, uncovering a zeal within me for communing with him through his word.

For example, through a methodical, line-by-line study of Exodus at our church, God taught me about the foundational outpouring of his love on sinners like me. How could I not be hooked? I learned that the first three feasts of Leviticus 23 perfectly align with Christ's death, burial, and resurrection. His word not only speaks; it delivers!

My sanctification has been a slow, arduous process through which Christ has used the chisel, fire, and shears of his word to hammer, mold, and prune one sinner into something of a saint. Like real, Italian plaster, biblical truth had been layered on my heart for years and years; yet only recently has it begun to take the form of any real art.

But that is the gift of the Holy Spirit at work. His timing is perfect. However much you want to know God, he wants you to know him much, much more: "Now to him who is able to do far more abundantly than all that we ask or think, according to the power at work within us, to him be glory in the church and in Christ Jesus throughout all generations, forever and ever. Amen" (Eph. 3:20 21).

Blessed is the man . . .
[whose] delight is in the law of the Lord,
    and on his law he meditates day and night.

Whoever feeds on me, he also will live because of me.

JOHN 6:57

May God give you intentionality to shape your weeks
with his word, ingenuity to shower your days with
his voice, and creativity to punctuate your life and
the lives of those around you with fresh routines for
regularly availing yourself of his life-giving words.

DAVID MATHIS
Habits of Grace

6

Feed Yourself Creatively

PLEASE DON'T MISUNDERSTAND: attending corporate worship every Sunday and hearing God's word in that setting is
not an excuse to stop reading your Bible. Far from it.

Instead, hearing God's word corporately should encourage
us to keep engaging with Scripture throughout the rest of the
week. After you have tasted the goodness of the Lord Jesus in
the presence of his gathered people, I hope that you are hungry
for more of him, and for his words.

The previous chapter is actually your excuse to get creative
when it comes to God's word. It is an appeal for you to enjoy
God in Scripture, both corporately *and* individually. It is an
invitation to be discontent with anything less than satisfaction
in Jesus, to reject boredom and apathy, and to heed God's
beckoning, gracious call for the good of your soul:

> Why do you spend your money for that which is not
>   bread,
>   and your labor for that which does not satisfy?

Listen diligently to me, and eat what is good,
and delight yourselves in rich food. (Isa. 55:2)

Listen. Eat what is good. Delight yourselves. The Lord invites us to feed on him.

Freshness with God

For years I had been using the same Bible reading plan. And it was a good one. It varied the genre of readings each day, dipping into both testaments and including psalms and proverbs along the way.[1] But I was bored with it, and I was becoming bored with my Bible too.

Something had to change. But I had used the same routine for so long that I didn't know *how* to make a change. And I didn't know if I should. Was something wrong with me that I was struggling to delight in God's word? Would it be wrong to abandon the plan? After all, it was getting me in my Bible. And if the plan was so good, then *what was the matter with me?*

I'm sure the answers to these questions are multilayered. We are whole people with complex, hungry hearts in complex human bodies, and we are up against many hindrances. Yet, however imperfect my intentions were, I genuinely wanted to seek Jesus through his word. I *wanted* to want to enjoy my Bible, and my Lord, again.

So, one evening when my senior pastor taught a class for our church on "a fresh, varied, and original walk with God," I was all ears. I needed help.

1 It is called the "Five Day Bible Reading Plan," and I still use it! https://www.fiveday biblereading.com.

And what I heard from him felt like freedom.

My pastor said something to the effect of, "There is no one 'right' way to meet with the Lord in Scripture. And if you find yourself getting bored with your routine, then switch it up." (All the type-A personalities in the room exhaled a sigh of relief.)

This was the wisdom and permission I needed to do something different. My pastor is a godly, older believer who has walked many decades with Jesus and spent many of his working hours in the word—and here he was advocating for *creativity*, not a one-size-fits-all approach to the idea of "quiet time."

In other words, he was telling us to feed and not just read.[2]

So, friends, consider this chapter a similar encouragement. If you are bored with your Bible and you don't know why; if you are tired from following the same plan (like I was) and you're wondering how to be hungry again for the word; if you feel discouraged from the pace of schedule, the needs of people, the call of distractions, and the overwhelm of possibilities; or if you are having trouble climbing out from the guilt hole of "supposed-to's," then this chapter is for you.

Feeding, Not Just Eating

Moms are masters of creatively feeding themselves. Sometimes I'm shoving crackers into a plastic baggie for the road, while

---

2 Pastor Colin Smith says, "Feeding is a lot more than reading. Feeding involves taking something good into yourself—absorbing it—so that it actually becomes part of you and is life-giving to you." From "Feeding on Christ," part of the "Watch Your Life" course on the Open the Bible for Leaders website. You can find the free course at https://leaders.openthebible.org/library/watch-your-life-178583/418017/about/.

other times I'm eating my food standing up as I put lunch on the table for my kids. Dinnertime is usually when I sit down to eat.

When it comes to hunger, the point is that we *eat*. Because we must. We can't function without feeding our bodies. As every mom knows, you can get by on thrown-together, quickly consumed and convenient snacks . . . for a while.

We need to eat, yes. But we also need to feed ourselves well. We need to savor meals, not just scarf down snacks.

Busy moms (and our kids) can get by on fast snacks and mini-meals for a time—but eventually our bodies beg us for something better. To operate, they need vitamins and nutrients, as well as a combination of protein, fat, and carbohydrates. The soul is similar: its health depends on both *what* we consume and *how* we consume it.

So far we've touched on the *what*: we do not live by bread alone but by every word from God's mouth (Matt. 4:4). Our souls will not be truly satisfied unless we nourish ourselves with God's life-giving words and feed our hunger with the goodness of his grace in Jesus (Ps. 107:9; John 6:57). We've also seen how appetite is a great indicator of the heart, and can be easily derailed by many worldly alternatives and hindrances.

What we consume on a day-to-day basis matters for our soul. *Are we consuming God's word, or are we taking in other things that cannot really satisfy us?*

Second, and equally vital, is *how* we are consuming God's word. Just as I can handle eating on-the-go for only a short time, so our souls can "snack on" Scripture only for a little while before they beg us for something more. Nibbling on

Scripture isn't bad or wrong; in my case, literal snacking keeps me alive! We will have days and seasons when snacking on Scripture is our lifeline, and that is fine and good—but we don't want it to be *final*. We want our snacking to make us hungry for the full, well-rounded meal, when we feast with our church family and then feed on the Lord in his word privately.

We want it to whet our appetites for something better.

The Key to Feeding: Meditation

When my husband eats, he doesn't just eat—he *inhales* his food. He says it's a proper-temperature thing; he wants his hot food hot and his cold food cold. I just nod my head. But I think he's missing out on a fuller enjoyment of his meals.

Like slowing down when we eat, meditation on God's word is the Spirit-led process of *enjoying* it. It usually involves reading a verse (or a small chunk of verses), making observations about it, asking questions (even really hard ones), making connections (within a particular verse itself and within its broader context), and then applying its truths to our hearts.

Or, following our metaphor, meditation is *feeding*, not just eating.

Professor and author Don Whitney, who has taught and written extensively on spiritual disciplines, believes that "meditation is the greatest single devotional need of most Christians, even among those who read the Bible daily." Here's why:

So much processes through our brains that if we don't absorb some of it, we will be affected by none of it.

And surely if we should absorb anything that courses through our thinking, it should be the inspired words from heaven. Without absorption of the water of God's Word, there's no quench of our spiritual thirst. Meditation is the means of absorption. . . . I would encourage you to make it your general rule to "read big and meditate small" every day.[3]

Whitney recommends spending 25 to 50 percent of our Bible intake in meditation.[4] For example, if you have twenty minutes to read Scripture, you might take five minutes to read a bigger passage, ten minutes to meditate on a small portion of that passage (perhaps a verse or two), and five minutes to pray. This principle has encouraged me to slow down, which doesn't come naturally to me, and to taste what I am consuming so I'm not just inhaling my spiritual food. It has helped me feed, not merely eat.

Whitney isn't pulling this exercise out of midair, though. He is making a claim based on what the Bible itself teaches. Over and over again, God extols meditation, connecting it to the "blessing" (or satisfaction) of his people. We see this as a theme woven throughout Psalm 119, a song that is all about loving God's word:

I will praise you with an upright heart
    when I learn your righteous rules. (Ps. 119:7)

3 Donald S. Whitney, *Ten Questions to Diagnose Your Spiritual Health* (Colorado Springs: NavPress, 2021), 19.
4 Whitney, *Ten Questions*, 19.

I will meditate on your precepts
    and fix my eyes on your ways.
I will delight in your statutes;
    I will not forget your word. (Ps. 119:15–16)

At midnight I rise to praise you,
    because of your righteous rules. (Ps. 119:62)

Oh how I love your law!
    It is my meditation all the day. (Ps. 119:97)

How sweet are your words to my taste,
    sweeter than honey to my mouth! (Ps. 119:103)

When we taste something amazing, we can't help but tell people about it. My husband and I love discovering restaurants and enjoying new foods and dishes together. If our experience is great, we usually end up praising the restaurant, writing a review, talking about how wonderful it was, and telling others about it. Our tasting leads to great delight.

This is what we see happening throughout Scripture (Ps. 119 in particular). Meditation on God's word is connected to delight in God's word. And delight in God's word leads us to hunger more for it, which leads us to meditate more on it. This is a wonderfully gracious cycle of joy that God has designed for his people.

And it is ours for the taking, if we will only choose to meditate.[5]

5 Remember that this is not a formula. As we saw in chapter 2, we are helpless to enjoy coming to God in his word apart from his supernatural help. But he also does not

TASTE and Meditate

What does meditation look like for God's hungry people with full lives?

I have been reading my Bible for years but still find myself pondering this question. Each of us will meditate differently depending on the season we're in; sometimes, we will enjoy lingering, lengthy meditation by ourselves, while other times we will need to get creative with feeding ourselves on Christ's word. Whether we are feasting with our church—a fantastic God-given means of built-in meditation alongside other hungry believers—or "snacking on" Scripture alongside our children, the point is that we feed our souls. I have personally benefited from Whitney's 25-to-50 percent principle. It has nourished my soul with more than a snack and helps me remember what I have read.

Whatever season you're in and however you are getting creative with Scripture intake, the following is one framework for meditation you might use. It follows the acronym TASTE: *think* about it, *ask* questions, *seek* Jesus, *take* away truth, and *enjoy* God.

Think about It

As you prayerfully read a portion of Scripture, whether a few chapters or a few verses, choose a key verse to focus your meditation on, something that stands out to you. You might choose to write a verse in a journal or journaling Bible, as writing helps

---

miraculously act in our hearts *apart* from coming to his word. God graciously uses means. This is why meditation and delight are connected.

us think more clearly. Repetition also promotes clear thinking, so you may want to reread the surrounding verses a few times. You are priming your mind and heart for what's to come.

Ask Questions

Once you have your verse identified and/or written down, get curious about it. Who was it originally written to, and why? What does it tell you about God, yourself, the church, the world, or the spiritual realm? What don't you understand about it? What connections can you make within the verse and with other parts of the Bible? What do certain words mean, and why did the author choose those words? After trying to answer your own questions, if you have the time you might consult a study Bible or commentary for added help.

Seek Jesus

In all our meditating, we want to remember that it is possible to search the Scriptures and miss the main character. And we don't want to miss Jesus! We want to discover him in all of God's word, calling upon the Spirit to help us see and love the Son. For he is the point of the whole Bible and all our meditation. You might prayerfully use the *five questions to look for Jesus* from chapter 3 as a guide.

Take Away Truth

This is what we might call application, or bringing the word home.[6] We want God's word to make a difference in our hearts

6   David Mathis, *Habits of Grace: Enjoying Jesus through the Spiritual Disciplines* (Wheaton, IL: Crossway, 2016), 62.

(James 1:25), so we ask him to change us. You might take away a specific application from the Spirit; or you might rest in knowing that he is conforming you into God's image by the word, whether you have a specific takeaway or not.[7] The point, remember, is *seeing and enjoying Jesus*, and growing in our hunger for him.

Enjoy God

In everything, our ultimate goal is to hunger for God and be satisfied in him. This is what we were made for. Since our hearts are naturally dull to the most delightful reality in the universe, the aim of meditation is to awaken our hearts to truest delight, to fullest satisfaction—to the glory of God in the face of Jesus Christ (2 Cor. 4:6)—so we would be discontent with anything less than him and hunger for him more. May our meditation on the Word, through the word, lead to love, praise, and increasing delight. May it lead us to enjoy God.

Satisfied Souls

Whether we are snacking or feasting on Scripture, we want our souls to be satisfied in the Lord. We want to seek God in fresh, creative ways that keep us hungering for him and for his words. Rejecting boredom and apathy in favor of delight and

7 I had not encountered this perspective until Mathis's excellent book. He writes: "Meditating on God's words shapes our soul. Sometimes that yields immediate and specific points of application—embrace them when they come. But be careful not to let the drive for specific actions alter the focus of our devotions from astonishment and seeking to have your soul happy in the Lord. Coming to the Scriptures to see and feel makes for a drastically different approach than primarily coming to do." Mathis, *Habits*, 64–65.

desire, we want to meditate on who God is and what he has done and make our souls happy in him.

So where can you start? Or how can you press on?

In the application section below, I have provided a list of ideas to feed yourself creatively with God's word. Some of these will feel more like snacking, while others will foster better and more prolonged meditation. But the point is that we not just eat but feed ourselves on the best food there is—the living words of the living God—so that our souls will be satisfied in him.

Feeding Yourself Creatively

By yourself:

- Use a Bible reading plan. You can find any of the following online:

  - 5x5x5 New Testament Bible Reading Plan
  - Five Day Bible Reading Plan
  - M'Cheyne Reading Plan
  - Two-Year Bible Reading Plan

- Print the Scripture reading on paper and meditate by marking it up.
- Journal portions of Scripture and meditate by marking it up.
- Read Scripture in the shower (insert a sheet of paper in an upside-down, gallon-sized baggie and tape it on the shower wall).[8]

8 Glenna Marshall, *Everyday Faithfulness: The Beauty of Ordinary Perseverance in a Demanding World* (Wheaton, IL: Crossway, 2020), 58–59.

- Listen to an audio Bible or app. You can listen while exercising, getting ready in the morning, doing chores, or driving. Some apps I recommend include Streetlights, Dwell, and the ESV Audio Bible.
- Leave your Bible open on the kitchen counter.
- Set reminders on your phone to meditate/memorize/pray.
- Set Scripture wallpapers on your phone, tablet, and computer.
- Listen to worship music that is based on Scripture.
- Listen to a sermon (and follow along in your Bible).
- Listen to podcasts that teach and meditate on Scripture. I recommend the following:

  - *The Bible Project*
  - *The Bible Recap* by D-Group
  - *The Deep Well with Erin Davis*
  - *Help Me Teach the Bible* with Nancy Guthrie
  - *In the Word, On the Go* with Champ Thornton
  - *Knowing Faith* by Kyle Worley, J. T. English, and Jen Wilkin
  - *Open the Bible* with Pastor Colin Smith
  - *The Ponder Podcast* with Laura Hardin
  - *She Reads Truth*
  - *Two Sisters and a Cup of Tea*

- Post Scripture verses around your house where you will see them.
- Write the first letters of words from a verse on your arm or hand (and try to memorize the verse based on the first letters).

With your family:

- Read a portion of Scripture during a meal and talk about it.

  - Make your way through a book of the Bible together.
  - Use a Bible reading plan.

- Use devotional resources that point to Scripture. For younger kids I recommend:

  - *The Biggest Story Storybook Bible* by Kevin DeYoung
  - *The Gospel Story Bible: Discovering Jesus in the Old and New Testaments* by Marty Machowski
  - *The Jesus Storybook Bible* by Sally Lloyd-Jones
  - *Kids Read Truth* products and flashcards
  - *The New City Catechism*
  - *The Promises of God Storybook Bible* by Jennifer Lyell
  - *Tales That Tell the Truth* picture books
  - *Tiny Theologians* products and flashcards

For older kids I recommend:

- *Emblems of the Infinite King: Enter the Knowledge of the Living God* by J. Ryan Lister
- *Epic Devotions: 52 Weeks in the Story That Changed the World* by Aaron Armstrong
- *Kaleidoscope Kids* Bibles
- *The-Ology: Ancient Truths Ever New* by Marty Machowski

- *Unfolding Grace for Kids: A 40-Day Journey through the Bible*
- *WonderFull: Ancient Psalms Ever New* by Marty Machowski

- Memorize verses together (you can even set them to rhythms or music).
- Listen to Scripture-based music:

  - Slugs and Bugs
  - Corner Room
  - Seeds Family Worship
  - Ellie Holcomb's kids' albums
  - Shane and Shane's kids' albums

- Sing worship music based on Scripture.
- Create artwork based on Bible verses.
- Listen to Bible-based podcasts:

  - *The Big Picture Podcast* by Crossway
  - *God's Big Story* by the Village Church
  - *Jesus Is Better: Bible Stories with Gospel Joy* with Alicia Yoder

With friends:

- Join a Bible-centered small group at your church.
- Use a Bible reading plan with a friend, and talk about it during the week.
- Read the Bible one-on-one with a friend or neighbor.
- Listen to sermons or podcasts and discuss.

- Read and discuss a Bible-based, Bible-saturated book.
- Memorize Scripture together, and hold each other accountable.
- Text Scripture to each other during the week.

Many Ways to Grow in God's Word

Bill (seventies, husband, father, grandfather, entrepreneur, and Bible study leader)

My first study in God's word began with a neighborhood Bible study. After I had attended a retreat called Seek Ye First the Kingdom of God (based on Matt. 6:33), our neighbors invited my wife and me to join their study of John's Gospel. Experiencing challenges in our young family, I was curious about seeking God first and setting right priorities, and my appetite for God's word began to grow.

A few years later my wife, Judy, encouraged me to join Bible Study Fellowship, a disciplined program that encourages daily time in the word. Through BSF and his word, God has developed within me a greater hunger to know him and apply his truth to my life.

Several years ago my wife and I committed to read God's word together. Choosing a book of the Bible to study, we take turns reading aloud, discuss what we read, and pray. This has been transformative in deepening our relationship with the Lord and with each other. The word of God has provided strength, wisdom, and hope for each day, and has encouraged us through a cancer diagnosis, heart attack, and family difficulties. This commitment to study the word and pray together has lasted twenty years!

Our recent study of Psalm 119, especially verse 144 ("Give me understanding that I may live"), has helped us navigate a confused world. In many ways, God's word is teaching us to trust him, and it has helped us replace fear and anxiety with peace and contentment.

I am watching over my word to perform it.

JEREMIAH 1:12

*God weaves even the seemingly failed hour
of study into the fabric of illumination.*

JOHN PIPER
Reading the Bible Supernaturally

*Our inner self is being renewed day by day.
. . . For the things that are seen are transient,
but the things that are unseen are eternal.*

2 CORINTHIANS 4:16, 18

7

Trust God's Nourishing Work

"IS THIS GOING to make any difference?"

Neither of us knew the answer to this question. My soon-to-be husband and I were debriefing my recent appointment with a homeopathic physician. After six years of increasing chronic pain and numerous visits to specialty doctors, I was getting desperate for answers. So far, the outcome of this visit seemed promising, but not without challenge.

My new course of action? A drastic change of diet.

And I mean drastic: I would have to eliminate gluten, dairy, grains, soy, legumes, and all forms of refined sugar. To know if it was making any difference, I would commit for two months and then evaluate the results via bloodwork and symptom-monitoring.

Adopting such a lifestyle was tough—my grocery expenses grew, food prep took longer, and eating out was difficult—but the promise of healing kept me going. With each day of commitment and sacrifice I wondered, *Is this making any difference?*

Everything felt so elusive. I could not see or feel the results. At least, not for some time.

More Than You Can See

Our engagement with God's word can feel like this (maybe more than we would like to admit). Surrounded by fast-paced days, needy family members, work responsibilities, and a million voices demanding our attention, we wonder if committing to Scripture is really worth it. *Does it make any difference*, we ask? And if it does, then why doesn't this difference seem more obvious to us?

I have thought this plenty of times, and have talked to many others who have too. We open our Bibles, pray, read, meditate, and pray again—only to get discouraged when our hearts feel unmoved. Ten minutes later, we find ourselves yelling at our kids or coworkers, and we begin to doubt the power of God's word. We lose hope when it seems our hunger for God has not grown, that we have not changed all that much, even through many years of taking in his words. Or perhaps we haven't been engaged with Scripture at all lately, and the idea of starting again overwhelms us. The whole thing seems either too good to be true, or not good enough to be worth it.

In this chapter, I want to encourage you that *when you engage with God's word, more is happening than you can see.*

Our constant opportunity, day in and day out, is to wait for the unseen, ongoing, and seemingly slow but always good work of God—which means waiting for God himself in his word. Waiting is never easy. But waiting *on the Lord* is worth it because it means trusting the one whose promises never fail and who delights to show himself trustworthy, especially to people like us who urgently need him to show up.

Nowhere Else to Go

I once entered a trying season of what I would call spiritual depression.[1] Our family had been sick on and off for close to a year, so we kept to ourselves; we stayed away from church and other people for a long time. The lingering Midwest winter was also wearing me down. And on top of it all, my husband and I lost a second baby to miscarriage.

The loneliness and grief of living in this fallen world felt suffocating.

As the dual clouds of sadness and longing settled upon my soul, I started to ask questions and face doubts about the Lord, an unwelcome battleground every believer enters at some point. I asked my small group to pray for the heaviness to break. I needed the light of Jesus to stream into my weary heart again.

I knew I needed his word more than anything else.

Yet, engaging with it was a struggle. I would approach the Lord in Scripture only to feel as if no one answered the door. The words on the page seemed to bounce off my heart rather than penetrate it. But I knew I had no other choice. I needed to be in the word.

So I committed to simply continue. No matter my detached feelings and how bleak circumstances seemed, I would come.

1   This is simply my own way of labeling and describing what I experienced. One of the best books I've read on this subject is Martyn Lloyd-Jones's *Spiritual Depression: Its Causes and Its Cure*.

I would plead and ask, and ask again. I remember praying along the lines of Jacob's prayer in Genesis 32:26: "I will not let you go unless you bless me." People were praying for me, and I knew the very words of life were mine to feed on, and *where else could I go*? "You have the words of eternal life" (John 6:68).

Eventually, on a normal day, through the normal means of his gracious words and prayerful people, the Lord met me. In his own supernatural way and in his own timing, he shined his light upon my heart again, and the clouds of heaviness began to disperse.

Longing for His Promise

I do not tell you this story because there is some magic formula for dealing with hardship (there isn't), or because I'm so great at committing to God's word (I'm not), but because God is so great at committing himself to us, *and we cannot know the trustworthiness of his commitment to us apart from his word*. His word is his commitment, his promise, and his covenant faithfulness that never ends (Ps. 119:76). To trust him is to trust what he has said, and our faith in him is strengthened as we hold fast to his word. And, oh, how we long for something trustworthy to cling to when everything else is changing, including us! The psalmist's plea was my own: "My eyes long for your promise; / I ask, 'When will you comfort me?'" (Ps. 119:82).

We too hunger for his promise, even without realizing it. Despite our many attempts to cover it up, we know we are needy at our core. In our hunger, combined with this passing-away world and its many troubles and tears, God graciously gives us something more sure for our faith-weary eyes to rest upon: *his words.* His unchanging, true, and powerful words.

We are visual creatures. We were made to see God (Gen. 3:8). The whole story of redemption is about God's people learning to walk with him by faith, not by sight (2 Cor. 5:7) until we see him, in the flesh, with our physical eyes (Col. 3:4). And though we cannot see him now, he sees us and knows us and sustains our faith with something we *can* see. *His words.*

He is so kind and good.

And yet, what his word produces within us is *unseen.* This is the hard part, I think, for needy, hungry souls like us who want something visible to hold onto day after day. So we need encouragement. The work of God through his word is supernatural, ongoing, and seemingly slow at times, but it is always trustworthy and good. In my cloud-laden season, God was not absent, nor was he idle. He was working in more ways that I can pinpoint even now. He was using it, "weaving" it into the "fabric of illumination," as John Piper beautifully puts it.[2]

God was using his word to shine his light so I could see again.

Coming to Truly See

When we come to the Bible, we come to truly *see.* We desperately need spiritual sight (faith)! Much of what we can physically see around us is hard, grievous, and hope-quenching. What our weary souls need more than anything in this world is to see reality God's way.

2   John Piper, *Reading the Bible Supernaturally: Seeing and Savoring the Glory of God in Scripture* (Wheaton, IL: Crossway, 2017), 292.

This is what the light of the word of Christ does. It illuminates. It shows us his glory. It shows us our need for his glory to be our greatest good, no matter what is happening around us or within us.

Friends, when we come to our Bibles (either privately or with our church family), we come to be reminded of a reality that is more real and powerful than the one visibly surrounding us, of a coming creation that makes the one outside our window pale in comparison, of a kingdom that cannot be shaken by rulers, wars, pandemics, or the stormy doubts inside our hearts. Through God's word of truth, we come to know and believe and hunger for the God who has made us for himself. Though he is a God we cannot see, he has given us eyes of faith and hearts of hope that are instilled by his words: "For God, who said, 'Let light shine out of darkness,' has shone in our hearts to give the light of the knowledge of the glory of God in the face of Jesus Christ" (2 Cor. 4:6).

Where do we gain knowledge about who God is, in all his glory? *In his Son, his Word.* And how do we "see" the face of Jesus Christ? *Through his word, the Bible.*

But how do we do this? How do we come to trust God's nourishing work, a work we can't always see, when the world around us and the emotions inside us tend to feel more real? How do we seek the light of Christ when the darkness seems to envelop us, even our very desire?

We obey, and we cling.

We Come to God's Word

First, we obey. Sometimes the word *obedience* makes us cringe. (Did you cringe?) It causes us to think legalistic thoughts and, if we aren't careful, we will slip into trying to earn God's love and approval by our actions. Yet, obedience is good, commanded by God, and commended in his word: "Strive . . . for the holiness without which no one will see the Lord" (Heb. 12:14). "Therefore, my beloved, as you have always obeyed . . . work out your own salvation with fear and trembling" (Phil. 2:12). Obedience is evidence of true faith in Jesus.

It demonstrates that we trust him enough to do what he says.

It demonstrates that we love him and actually want to know him.

It demonstrates that we acknowledge that, without him, we would be lost.

And so we come to his word. No matter how we feel or how things appear, we come. We choose to believe that the way of obedience is the way of life, which is how parents instruct their children, that it may go well with them (Eph. 6:1–3). We choose to believe that God works through our obedience, using it to nourish us with his words and fill us with himself.

The unexpected blessing is that *obedience both proves our faith and produces more faith*, helping us cling all the more tightly to God's promises as we obey him, just as it did for Abraham.

We Cling to God's Word

Abraham was in an impossible situation, or so it seemed. He and his wife were old—really old—and well beyond childbearing years. And yet, God told them they would have a son, from whom God's entire family line would come. Even though God's promise seemed impossible, Abraham "[trusted] God, and it was counted to him as righteousness" (Gen. 15:6; Rom. 4:3).

Abraham obeyed, giving God glory, and "he grew strong in his faith" (Rom. 4:20) as a result.

We too desire stronger faith. Deep in our hearts, we need to be convinced, as Abraham was, that God's words are not just hot air—empty, lifeless, and cheap. No, God's words are purposeful, nourishing, and invaluable. They are worth trusting, for God's words come from God's heart. We cling to them because God is the only trustworthy, unchanging rock upon which we can stand. And so we keep coming to God's word, and we keep clinging to the promises we find there. As Abraham did.

What are some of those promises? At the end of this chapter, I've included a list of promises related specifically to the work of God's word. When we cling to his promises about his word, God gets the glory and praise, since in our waiting upon him we are proclaiming *him* to be trustworthy and worth the wait, not the things of this world. In clinging, we remind ourselves, other people, and even the spiritual realm that the unseen, ongoing, seemingly slow work of God is always good, that there is more happening than we can now see and observe with our eyes, and that God is nourishing us even when we can't feel it.

Nourishing Our Souls

Just as I couldn't see the difference that each day of regimented eating was making to my weak health, so it is often hard to assess the work of God in our weary souls as we obediently and desperately consume his word. But the right eating lifestyle was changing me. Little by little, the doctor's plan was unfolding its good purpose.

And little by little, one day at a time, God is working his good purpose within us.

Even when we can't see it.

He is working through his word, satisfying our hunger and nourishing our souls with his words of life, the food we need the very most.

Trusting God's Nourishing Work

What does God promise about the work of his word? What can we trust him for as we obediently seek him in it? Here are a list of promises to cling to as you engage with Scripture (and there are many, many more).

God's Word Is Alive

For the word of God is living and active, sharper than any two-edged sword, piercing to the division of soul and of spirit, of joints and of marrow, and discerning the thoughts and intentions of the heart. (Heb. 4:12)

God's Word Gives Wisdom

From childhood you have been acquainted with the sacred writings, which are able to make you wise for salvation through faith in Christ Jesus. (2 Tim. 3:15; see also Prov. 2:6–7)

God's Word Equips Us for Good Works

All Scripture is breathed out by God and profitable for teaching, for reproof, for correction, and for training in righteousness, that the man of God may be complete, equipped for every good work. (2 Tim. 3:16–17)

God's Word Is Purposeful

For as the rain and the snow come down from heaven
  and do not return there but water the earth,
making it bring forth and sprout,
  giving seed to the sower and bread to the eater,
so shall my word be that goes out from my mouth;
  it shall not return to me empty,
but it shall accomplish that which I purpose,
  and shall succeed in the thing for which I sent it.
    (Isa. 55:10–11)

God's Word Makes Us Holy

Sanctify them in the truth; your word is truth. (John 17:17)

God's Word Brings Blessing

Blessed is the man
  who walks not in the counsel of the wicked,
nor stands in the way of sinners,
  nor sits in the seat of scoffers;
but his delight is in the law of the Lord,
  and on his law he meditates day and night. (Ps. 1:1–2;
    see also Prov. 2:20)

God's Word Cannot Fail

Not one word of all the good promises that the Lord had made to the house of Israel had failed; all came to pass. (Josh. 21:45)

God's Word Is a Safe Place

This God—his way is perfect;
    the word of the LORD proves true;
    he is a shield for all those who take refuge in him.
        (2 Sam. 22:31; see also Ps. 18:30)

God's Word Brings Comfort

This is my comfort in my affliction,
    that your promise gives me life. (Ps. 119:50)

God's Word Gives Peace

Great peace have those who love your law;
    nothing can make them stumble. (Ps. 119:165)

God's Word Instructs and Leads

Good and upright is the LORD;
    therefore he instructs sinners in the way.
He leads the humble in what is right,
    and teaches the humble his way. (Ps. 25:8–9)

God's Word Gives Understanding

The unfolding of your words gives light;
    it imparts understanding to the simple.
        (Ps. 119:130)

God's Word Kills Sin and Defeats Evil

Oh, that my people would listen to me,
    that Israel would walk in my ways!

I would soon subdue their enemies
  and turn my hand against their foes. (Ps. 81:13–14)

God's Word Brings Confidence

I bless the LORD who gives me counsel;
  in the night also my heart instructs me.
I have set the LORD always before me;
  because he is at my right hand, I shall not be shaken.
    (Ps. 16:7–8)

God's Word Gives Joy

The precepts of the LORD are right,
  rejoicing the heart. (Ps. 19:8)

God's Word Creates and Sustains

He upholds the universe by the word of his power.
(Heb. 1:3)

God's Word Protects

The steps of a man are established by the LORD,
  when he delights in his way;
though he fall, he shall not be cast headlong,
  for the LORD upholds his hand. (Ps. 37:23–24)

God's Word Brings Life

Keep hold of instruction; do not let go;
  guard her, for she is your life. (Prov. 4:13)

God's Power, Our Persistence

Linda (seventies, wife, mother, grandmother, retiree, and small group leader)

I grew up in an unchurched home. Soon after I was saved (at age forty-seven), I came to understand the power of Scripture when dealing with panic attacks. I realized that if I could "reroute" my mind from the growing fear that those attacks generated, I could short-circuit them. By God's grace (and using a concordance), I wrote out verses about worry, fear, and anxiety. I carried those cards with me at all times and used them when I felt a panic attack taking hold. Over time, the panic attacks lessened and then dissipated—and I was left with the blessing of verses that I had memorized.

The desire to continue to memorize Scripture was born.

As I have gotten older, memorizing has become more difficult, but I know that with persistence and time, it is well worth the effort. As more of God's word gets into me, it fuels my desire to grow in learning how to live under its authority. I have also learned that there will be things in the word I won't understand—at least in the present time. Embracing that has taught me to be content with where God has me and with what he has chosen to reveal to me. As I grow to know him more fully through his word, I am also better able to make decisions that honor him.

I have learned the importance of having regular time in the word, of memorizing it at a pace that is sustainable for me, of being in small groups, Bible studies, and relationships with godly, Christian women of all ages, and of regularly attending weekly worship services—all of these have been vital to my walk with the Lord.

I have also learned that there are things he has designed for me to do in his process of sanctification, and things that only *he* can do. I trust him to orchestrate the process of making me more like Jesus and equipping me for the good work he has prepared for me. I know he will be faithful to do that for you as well, as you continually entrust yourself to him.

In the heart of every human being is
stamped a feeling for divinity.

JOHN CALVIN
Institutes of the Christian Religion

Your words were found, and I ate them,
and your words became to me a joy
and the delight of my heart.

JEREMIAH 15:16

Therefore they are before the throne of God,
and serve him day and night in his temple;
and he who sits on the throne will shelter them with
his presence.
They shall hunger no more, neither thirst anymore.

REVELATION 7:15–16

8

Embrace Your Hunger

"DO YOU WANT to go away as well?"

Jesus addressed this question to his disciples—the ones who were left, at least. Many had already walked away from him because his message was not always easy to hear. His words cut to the heart. So he asked those closest to him now to think about the cost of following him. They did not yet know how hard things would get, how tightly they would need to hold on. They would need each other. They would need his words.

They would need Jesus to hold on to them.

And so he turned to the twelve disciples and asked them his question: *"Do you want to go away as well?"* (John 6:67).

Simon Peter replied, "Lord, to whom would we go? You have the words that give eternal life. We believe, and we know you are the Holy One of God" (John 6:68–69 NLT).

Hardship and Hunger

As we wrap up this book about growing our appetite for God's word, the question on my mind is, *Where do we go from here?* How do we keep pursuing something that can feel so unfinished and imperfect in this life, namely, the satisfying of our deepest hunger in Jesus and in his nourishing words, especially when life is hard?

At the end of a book like this one, it's natural for us to want a straightforward list of how-to's, a surefire plan for change. And while I hope these chapters have helped and encouraged you toward a greater desire for Scripture, no book can do what only God can in the human heart. Only he can increase our appetite for his words *through* his word. So we put ourselves in the position to receive from him, again and again. We ask him to do a supernatural miracle within us through his word.

And we let the many hardships of our days make us needy.

So where do we go from here? We learn to embrace our hunger, letting it drive us to the only source of fullness, our true bread. We learn to see suffering, of whatever form or degree, as a strangely wrapped gift to be received from God's hand, a reminder to us of reality: we are hungry for him.

This may seem obvious, but it's hard for us to accept. Why? We don't like to be needy. And it doesn't feel natural to embrace anything that exposes our need.

Neediness is evidence of our weakness, vulnerability, and discomfort. It is proof that we can't supply everything for ourselves, that we are more hungry than we realize and more dependent than we like to admit. The world's embrace of autonomy and its rejection of authority naturally dwells within each of us—but no matter where we run or what we do, nothing will stop the perpetual need, the lingering hunger within our souls.

It is there, gnawing at our pride and reminding us we aren't home yet.

We are in the wilderness. And we are hungry.

The beautiful thing about the story of the Bible is its realism. Scripture does not provide an escape from reality, but enters right into it. If you feel like every day is a struggle, you're right; it is. If you feel like your desires are messed up (even those related to the Bible) and that you can't get your act together, you're right; they are, and you can't. From the garden throughout the generations, God's word has told us the tale of the human soul: our wholehearted hunger for the Creator, our terrible plunge into starvation, and our countless attempts to fix and fill ourselves with anything but true bread. We are in the wilderness, indeed.

But here's the good news: *God's word is for the wilderness,* for those not yet home.

It is for you and for me. It is for the hungry.

Every hardship—whether obvious and acute suffering, or the daily, lingering futility we all feel—is readying us for Jesus. Every groan anticipates glory. Every hunger pang points us to heaven.

So as we ponder together where to go from here, let's look at two wilderness accounts from Scripture—two stories that instruct us about embracing our hunger today.

Grumbling and Grace

God's people had just seen a body of water divide at Moses's command, creating an escape route through the Red Sea. They had hurried through safely on foot, and not one life was lost—that is, until the waves came crashing down on their pursuers.

This was a miraculous salvation. An undeserved deliverance from death.

But now they had food on their minds. As they entered the wilderness, the whole congregation of Israel grumbled against Moses and his brother Aaron. "If only the LORD had killed us back in Egypt," they moaned. "There we sat around pots filled with meat and ate all the bread we wanted. But now you have brought us into this wilderness to starve us all to death" (Ex. 16:3 NLT).

How could they, we wonder?

Yet, we too forget. We have seen God deliver our souls from starving hunger. We were on the brink of spiritual death, oppressed by sin and selfishness and enslaved by worldly desires. But when hardship comes to us—an unexpected health crisis, the death of a family member, extended strain from job loss, the darkness of depression, daily disappointments, the brokenness of everything—we are more like the Israelites than we'd like to admit.

We're forgetful, turning from God and his word. We ask, Will he come through?

Does he really care for me? Is he everything he says he is? Is his word really that trustworthy?

As we walk through our own wilderness, it's easy to think that the removal of hardship would make everything better. "If only _____ would go away or improve, then I would be happy." "If only _____ would change, then I could get into my Bible." Perhaps our circumstances *would* be easier—no one prefers pain and hardship—but an easy life doesn't guarantee a satisfied soul.

The wilderness exposes our need for the word.

Often, God uses our hunger to reveal more of his perfect ability to fill it. And often God fills us with himself even when we don't intend to be satisfied with him. He keeps giving us his word even when we grumble. This is called grace.

In Exodus 16, the word *grumble* is used multiple times. The people grumble against Moses and Aaron, which is ultimately a grumbling against the Lord. And how does the Lord respond to their complaining? "I have heard the grumbling of the people of Israel. Say to them, 'At twilight you shall eat meat, and in the morning you shall be filled with bread. Then you shall know that I am the Lord your God'" (Ex. 16:12).

God responds with grace. He gives the people what they do not deserve, passing over their grumbling and providing them with daily bread. This is striking. In our daily struggle to hunger for God's word as we should, in all our wayward desires and distractedness, *God still provides what we need most.* He gives us himself through the daily manna of our Bibles, through an encounter with his Son brought about graciously by his Spirit.

We grumble. God gives.

This is who he is for us in the wilderness, friends. We may wonder if our appetite for God and his words has grown at all over the years; we will struggle with discouragement and failure, even as we pursue such growth; we may be plunged into a depth of suffering that makes us question whether God's promises are true, if he is really for us after all; we may be tempted to turn from him to lesser things.

But he doesn't turn from us. Instead, he continues to give us himself. He speaks, that we may know that he is the Lord our God. Even when we grumble, even when we turn away, he provides.

Good Works and Good News

Fast-forward 1,200 years. Jesus lifts up his eyes from the mountain and sees a large crowd coming toward him (John 6). It had been a long week of ministry for his disciples, and they were not yet called to rest. There was more work to be done, more people to help.

More grace to be given.

So Jesus turns to Philip and asks, "Where are we to buy bread, so that these people may eat?" (6:5).

Flustered, the disciples look at each other, sure that no amount of money would be enough to feed a crowd like this. Andrew volunteers a small boy's lunch—five loaves of bread and two fish—but he is also making a point. There just isn't enough to go around.

Or so they think.

Jesus tells his disciples to have the people sit down in the grass. And he does what he alone can do. He feeds them. By a miraculous multiplication, he feeds the crowd. And not just barely, but abundantly—so abundantly that there are leftovers. So abundantly that the crowds start following him around, wanting more of what he has to give.

"We want to perform God's works, too. What should we do?" his followers ask him. Jesus takes this opportunity to correct their idea of what a good work is, of what their souls need most: "This is the only work God wants from you: Believe in the one he has sent" (John 6:29 NLT).

Believe. This is also what Jesus wants most from us, friends. He wants our hearts.

Just as the crowds did, we often think we can earn God's approval by performing the necessary "good works" of the Christian life, including Bible reading. We wrongly conclude that we have to "get this right" in order for God to love us. And if we don't get it right? Then we must not be serious enough, holy enough, or good enough. And so we try harder; we get up earlier; we study longer—only to find ourselves more tired and discouraged than when we began. And as the guilt presses in, it's easy to want to give up.

Like the forgetful crowds we anxiously ask, "What should we *do*?"

But this book, friends, has not been about doing everything right as it pertains to your Bible. It has not been about working your way toward some kind of "good Christian" status in God's eyes, or in the eyes of others, through the way you engage with Scripture. None of us are good enough for God and his grace, and that is the whole point. That is precisely why we run to his word: to receive from him what we cannot provide for ourselves. All of us are hungry, needy, and desperate, and only Jesus can give us what we most need. *Himself.* All is grace.

This is what he told the crowds that day, and it is also good news for us:

I am the bread of life; whoever comes to me shall not hunger, and whoever believes in me shall never thirst. . . . All that the Father gives me will come to me, and whoever comes to me I will never cast out. For I have come down from heaven, not to do my own will but the will of him who sent me. And this is the will of him who sent me, that I should lose nothing of all that he has given me, but raise it up on the last day. (John 6:35–39)

No matter what your Bible reading track record has been, if you have come to Christ for the eternal life he alone can give, you are safe. He will never cast you out. If you have taken hold of Jesus by faith, admitting your helplessness and humbling yourself before him, then you can rest assured he will never, never let you go—no matter how messy your attempts to grow.

Has it been years since you opened your Bible? *Come to him.* It is never too late to start.

Has your heart been cold toward his words? *Come to him.* He creates burning hearts.

Have you been plagued by doubts and fear? *Come to him.* His promises are trustworthy.

Are you hungry? *Come to him.* He will fill you. He will give you life through his words.

Feasting Forever

So where do we go from here?

We keep admitting how hungry we are, embracing that hunger and letting it drive us to Jesus and his word, again and again. We remember that no amount of "right Bible reading" will save us. Only Jesus saves. We encounter him through Scripture, where his Spirit works to fill our souls with lasting satisfaction in him (John 6:63).

We remember the Holy One who, in the wilderness, fought every temptation and hardship by fully embracing the words of God (Luke 4:1–13), and we rejoice that he reigns in heaven to help us right now. We walk through the wilderness with him alongside us, as he beckons us to take up his word, trust his work, and embrace his heart.

As Jesus asked his friends, so he asks us: "Do you want to go away as well?"

No, Lord. Where else can we go?

Jesus has the words of eternal life as he feeds our hungry souls today and promises to feast with us on the last day, and forever.

Embracing Your Hunger

Here are four considerations as you move on from this book.

1. Consider the situations in which you are tempted to neglect (or reject) God's word. Think about your response to suffering, disappointment, doubt, and the daily groanings of your heart. What would you lose by turning away from Scripture? What would you gain by staying in the word? Hear Jesus asking you each morning, "Do you want to go away as well?" and imagine him waiting for you in his word.

2. Consider your responsibility to love your neighbor as yourself. What might others gain by your endurance in the word, especially when they are struggling to endure? How might you feed others when they can't feed themselves, just as Jesus and his disciples fed the crowd? Your Bible intake is not just for your own soul, but also for the eternal good of others.

3. Consider the power of habit in embracing your hunger for God. Food is one thing we habitually eat, and just as we consistently nourish our bodies with it, so we can habitually and consistently nourish our souls in God's word. How can you make Scripture a habit, a normal and expected part of your everyday routine? (See appendix 1 "How to Get Started" for some ideas.)

4. *Consider the coming feast of the Lamb.* Someday soon, Jesus will come back, transforming the whole creation (including us) and welcoming all his people to the wedding feast of heaven. Every "meal" we eat with him now prepares us for this, and we will enjoy it all the more as we enjoy him today. Don't wait—anticipate the eternal feast by coming to the table!

Appendix 1

How to Get Started Reading Your Bible

I WANT TO READ my Bible more, but I don't know where to start.

This is a common struggle. The Bible is a large and daunting volume made up of sixty-six different books, 1,189 chapters, more than thirty-one thousand verses, and a host of genres including narrative, history, poetry, prophecy, proverb, allegory, and legal writings. Whew! No wonder we don't know how to get going.

But the best way to start is to *start*.

The best way to grow your appetite for Scripture is to begin feeding on it. That said, here is a brief guide to help you begin engaging with your Bible.

Make a Commitment

We all have good intentions—but intentions are only as good as the actions we take to fulfill them. It is one thing to think, *I'd like to read my Bible more.* It is quite another to make a commitment to do so, and then follow through with it. Verbalize your commitment before God in prayer, and ask for his help to keep you going even when it gets hard. (You can also write your commitment down in a journal where you can physically see it and return to it.) Then, verbalize your commitment to a spouse, family member, pastor, or trusted friend, someone who can check with you about how it's going, hold you accountable, and pray for you.

Greet the Day

There is no biblical command about reading Scripture in the morning, but there is a wise principle attached to it: we have not yet been conformed to the world and have a fresh opportunity to be transformed by the renewing of our minds before the day begins (Rom. 12:2). We also see examples in Scripture of people seeking the face of God first thing in the morning:

- Isaiah writes, "Morning by morning he awakens; / he awakens my ear to hear as those who are taught" (Isa. 50:4).
- Moses prays, "Satisfy us in the morning with your steadfast love, / that we may rejoice and be glad all our days" (Ps. 90:14).
- Mark's Gospel says about Jesus, "And rising very early in the morning, while it was still dark, he departed and went out to a desolate place, and there he prayed" (Mark 1:35).

Again, starting your day with Scripture is not a command, only a recommendation for preparing your mind and heart for the day. If mornings are hard for you—if you struggle to sleep at night or your work requires you to start early—then leverage whatever time you can find, even if it's midday or before bed. What matters is your pursuit of Jesus, not the practical details.

Start Small

When it comes to Bible reading, I don't recommend starting with a BHAG (a "big hairy audacious goal") but rather with a *realistic* goal. So, instead of saying you will wake up one hour earlier every day and spend that hour studying a passage, you might aim to set your alarm five minutes earlier for one week and enjoy meditating on a verse. The following week, set your alarm five minutes earlier, and so on, until your body adjusts and you're happy with your new starting time. Small adjustments can bring meaningful change.

Similarly, rather than setting out to read the whole Bible in one year (which is fantastic, but can be defeating if you get behind), start with smaller sections of Scripture. You can make your way through one book at a time, a few verses at a time; or you can use a plan, but take as much time as you need with it. Most study Bibles contain reading plans, or you can find them for free online. You might also ask your pastor for suggestions about where to begin reading. Choose a Bible study with a workbook or study questions that guide you into a text.

Every deposit you make, no matter how small, adds up.

Create a Habit

We are creatures of habit, thriving on routine. And just like we habitually eat, so we want to habitually feed our souls. If possible, choose a time and place that can stay (mostly) the same every day. You might even set up a space before the time begins so it is welcoming and ready for you. Try committing yourself to this new habit for thirty days, and see what happens.

One important habit I recommend is "Bible before screens." Our phones and computers are distracting tools vying for our attention, so it is beneficial for us to leave them alone until after we've spent time with God in his word.

Of course, there are seasons when our habits get thrown off and we need a change of plan. Don't hesitate to mix it up and get creative. Habit is less about the *how* and more about the *what*. The point is that we prioritize food for our souls, so much so that we can't *not* enjoy God's word.

Don't Read Alone

Sometimes, reading the Bible is best done in company. Not only does this hold us accountable to the commitment we've made, but it also brings wisdom and insight we might not otherwise have gained while reading alone. Maybe you and a friend could follow the same reading plan and study and talk about it along the way; or maybe you could meet up in person and read Scripture side by side. Bible-based small groups at church are also great ways to get started. There is multiplied joy in meditating on God's precious word together.

Ask God for Help

As we've seen throughout this book, reading the Bible to encounter Jesus is a supernatural work of the Spirit. So we approach the word prayerfully, asking God to help us stick with it and see him more clearly as we read. (See the prayers at the end of chap. 2). The point is, we need God's help!

Appendix 2

Reading Lists

HAVE YOU EVER WONDERED whether the Bible is reliable, or how it came to be one, singular book? Do you need ideas for Bible study methods? The following is a list of excellent books about (1) the nature and trustworthiness of the Bible, (2) how to approach and engage the Bible, and (3) how to study the Bible. This list is by no means exhaustive, but will give you a start. Happy reading![1]

On the Nature and Trustworthiness of the Bible

- *The Doctrine of the Word of God* by John Frame (P&R, 2010)
- *The Inspiration and Authority of the Bible* by B. B. Warfield (P&R, 2020)
- *Knowing Scripture* by R. C. Sproul (IVP, 2009)
- *A Peculiar Glory: How the Christian Scriptures Reveal Their Complete Truthfulness* by John Piper (Crossway, 2016)

---

1   I have not personally read all of these books, but they have either been recommended to me by people I trust or been created by trustworthy authors and publishers.

- *Scribes and Scripture: The Amazing Story of How We Got the Bible* by John D. Meade and Peter J. Gurry (Crossway, 2022)
- *Taking God at His Word: Why the Bible Is Knowable, Necessary, and Enough, and What That Means for You and Me* by Kevin DeYoung (Crossway, 2014)
- *Unbreakable: What the Son of God Said about the Word of God* by Andrew Wilson (10Publishing, 2014)
- *Why Trust the Bible?* by Greg Gilbert (Crossway, 2015)

On How to Approach and Engage the Bible

- *Asking the Right Questions: A Practical Guide to Understanding and Applying the Bible* by Matthew S. Harmon (Crossway, 2017)
- *Before You Open Your Bible: Nine Heart Postures for Approaching God's Word* by Matt Smethurst (10Publishing, 2019)
- *Bible Delight* by Christopher Ash (Christian Focus, 2021)
- *The Epic Story of the Bible: How to Read and Understand God's Word* by Greg Gilbert (Crossway, 2022)
- *Even Better Than Eden: Nine Ways the Bible's Story Changes Everything about Your Story* by Nancy Guthrie (Crossway, 2018)
- *The God Who Is There: Finding Your Place in God's Story* by D. A. Carson (Baker, 2010)
- *Habits of Grace: Enjoying Jesus through the Spiritual Disciplines* by David Mathis (Crossway, 2016)

- *How to Read the Bible through the Jesus Lens: A Guide to Christ-Focused Reading of Scripture* by Michael Williams (Zondervan, 2012)
- *Open the Bible in 30 Days* by Colin Smith (Moody, 2020)
- *Reading the Bible Supernaturally: Seeing and Savoring the Glory of God in Scripture* by John Piper (Crossway, 2017)
- *Spiritual Disciplines for the Christian Life* by Donald S. Whitney (NavPress, 1991)
- *Time Well Spent: A Practical Guide to Developing Your Daily Devotions* by Colin Webster (10Publishing, 2021)

On How to Study the Bible

- *Dig Deeper: Tools for Understanding God's Word* by Andrew Sach and Nigel Beyond (Crossway, 2010)
- *How to Eat Your Bible: A Simple Approach to Learning and Loving the Word of God* by Nate Pickowicz (Moody, 2021)
- *How to Get the Most from God's Word: An Everyday Guide to Enrich Your Study of the Bible* by John MacArthur (W Publishing, 1997)
- *How to Read the Bible for All Its Worth* by Gordon D. Fee and Douglas Stuart (Zondervan, 1981)
- *How to Study Your Bible: Discover the Life-Changing Approach to God's Word* by Kay Arthur, David Arthur, and Pete De Lacy (Harvest House, 1994)
- *Literarily: How Understanding Bible Genres Transforms Bible Study* by Kristie Anyabwile (Moody, 2022)

- *One-to-One Bible Reading* by David Helm (Matthias Media, 2011)
- *Women of the Word: How to Study the Bible with Both Our Hearts and Our Minds* by Jen Wilkin (Crossway, 2014)

Acknowledgments

WHEN FINISHING A BOOK about growing our appetites for God's word, naturally I have to thank all those who have encouraged me toward this end over the years.

My parents raised us in a home built on the Bible, a gracious and invaluable gift of God to my sister and me. Thank you for believing and loving God's word, Mom and Dad.

Over eight years of marriage, my husband (and my pastor), Brad, has deepened my trust and delight in Scripture through his morning-by-morning commitment to abide in Jesus, his faithfulness to study well and preach with joy, and his conviction to live for Christ's glory. I love the way you love God's word (and us!). Thanks for cheering me on in this project and for being my best editor.

Our church, The Orchard, is committed to proclaiming the gospel through the word of Christ. Through the preaching and teaching of our pastors and staff, my awe for Jesus and his authoritative, life-giving words has grown. I am so thankful God led me to our church!

Thank you to my LIFE Group for the example you have set in pursuing Jesus together through his word. When I have been discouraged, doubtful, and overwhelmed, you have fed me the word of God and encouraged me to keep going. Thank you for your commitment to God, to our church, and to me, and for the many prayers you have prayed as I worked on this book. I love you all.

I also think about the many wise and gifted Bible teachers and fellow writers (too many to be named) whose books, studies, and friendship I have benefited from over the years. I am grateful to God for your influence and godly example in loving his word.

A few generous people kindly read drafts of this book, offering feedback and insights that have made it stronger. Huge thanks to my husband, my mom, Lydia Clevenger, Lauren Washer, and Callie Mascetti for your time, thoughts, and friendship.

To my kids, Joanna and John: I pray every day that you will love Jesus and his word above all else! I love how we get into the word together, and your eagerness and curiosity always encourage me toward a childlike faith. I love you both with all my heart.

To Don Gates: thank you for your hard work on my behalf and ultimately for Christ. I appreciate you.

To Todd, Tara, and the team at Crossway: you have made a dream come true in allowing me the privilege of writing *Help for the Hungry Soul*. Your books have deepened my hunger for the Bible over the years, and I am humbled to contribute. Thank you for believing in this project. Thank you for making it stronger!

Above all, to Jesus, my true bread, the Word made flesh: I can't wait to feast with you. Thank you for waiting for me every day in your word. There is nowhere else I can go. I love you, Lord.

General Index

Scripture Index